DAY TRADING FOR BEGINNERS

A GUIDE TO LEARN THE BEST STRATEGIES AND ADVANCED TECHNIQUES IN DAY AND SWING TRADING. INCLUDING STOCKS AND OPTIONS

BY JOHN SCOTT

© **Copyright 2019 - All rights reserved.**

The content contained within this book may not be reproduced, duplicated or transmitted without direct written permission from the author or the publisher.
Under no circumstances will any blame or legal responsibility be held against the publisher, or author, for any damages, reparation, or monetary loss due to the information contained within this book. Either directly or indirectly.

Legal Notice:

This book is copyright protected. This book is only for personal use. You cannot amend, distribute, sell, use, quote or paraphrase any part, or the content within this book, without the consent of the author or publisher.

Disclaimer Notice:

Please note the information contained within this document is for educational and entertainment purposes only. All effort has been executed to present accurate, up to date, and reliable, complete information. No warranties of any kind are declared or implied. Readers acknowledge that the author is not engaging in the rendering of legal, financial, medical or professional advice. The content within this book has been derived from various sources. Please consult a licensed professional before attempting any techniques outlined in this book.

By reading this document, the reader agrees that under no circumstances is the author responsible for any losses, direct or indirect, which are incurred as a result of the use of information contained within this document, including, but not limited to, — errors, omissions, or inaccuracies.

Table of Contents

INTRODUCTION: 7
CHAPTER 1: WHAT IS DAY TRADING? 12
CHAPTER 2: BASICS CONCEPTS OF DAY TRADING 17
CHAPTER 3: THE BEST STRATEGIES 23
CHAPTER 4: RULES FOR SUCCESSFUL DAY TRADING 26
CHAPTER 5: DAY TRADING VS. SWING TRADING 30
CHAPTER 6: FINANCIAL INSTRUMENTAL FOR SWING TRADING 36
CHAPTER 7: SWING TRADING GUIDING PRINCIPLES 42
CHAPTER 8: SWING TRADING STRATEGIES 46
CHAPTER 9: STOCKS AND OPTION TRADING 50
CHAPTER 10: HOW DOES DAY TRADING ACTUALLY WORK 56
CHAPTER 11: SELECTING A BROKER 60
CHAPTER 12: DAY TRADING TIPS FOR BEGINNERS 65
CHAPTER 13: PSYCHOLOGY AND MINDSET 70
CHAPTER 14: WHAT SHOULD YOU INVEST IN TO BE PROFITABLE AT DAY TRADING 74
CHAPTER 15: THE DOS AND DON'TS OF DAY TRADING 79
CHAPTER 16: TRENDS 83
CHAPTER 17: MONEY MANAGEMENT 87
CHAPTER 18: MAKE YOUR FIRST TRADE 93
CHAPTER 19: COMMON DAY TRADING MISTAKES TO AVOID 98
CHAPTER 20: BEST SOFTWARE FOR DAY TRADING 103
CHAPTER 21: CANDLESTICK PATTERNS 110
CHAPTER 22: PAPER TRADING; PRACTICING BEING A SKILLFUL TRADER 115

CHAPTER 23: RISK MANAGEMENT **120**
CHAPTER 24: RETAIL VS INSTITUTIONAL TRADERS **125**
CHAPTER 25: PORTFOLIO DIVERSIFICATION **129**
CHAPTER 26 - THE 3 M'S OF TRADING **135**
CONCLUSION: **139**

Introduction

Day trading is a great career option for the right person in the right circumstances. It requires a strong, decisive personality who wants to be running the show every step of the way. And because those profits aren't steady, good day traders have some financial cushion and good personal support systems to get them through the tough times.

Day trading is like owning any small business. You're the boss and you call the shots. Each day's successes — and failures — are due to you and you alone. The market is irrelevant because you can't control it. Working by yourself all day, you're responsible for everything from the temperature in the office to the functioning of the computers to the accounting for trades.

Good day traders are independent. They don't want someone to tell them what to do; they want to figure it out for themselves. They love a challenge, whether it's finding a good bargain on office supplies or developing a profitable way to arbitrage currency prices.

If you would like to work for yourself and control your own destiny, keep reading. Day trading may be for you.

As a day trader, you have the luxury of setting up shop wherever you please. All you need is an account with an online brokerage firm and high-speed Internet access. You don't even need a computer if you have a smart phone. Nowadays you can find these tools almost anywhere: at home, at the library, in a bar, in a big city, in a small town, in the mountains, or in another country. Day trading offers a lot of geographic flexibility, which few other businesses do. You can trade while traveling as easily as you would trade at home — especially with improved mobile services.

The financial-services industry was one of the first to embrace computer technology in a big way, back in the 1960s, and it is still a technology-intensive industry. The people in colored cotton jackets running around the exchange floor, waving their hands and yelling at each other, are anachronisms.

Day traders use software to develop and refine their trading strategies. They trade online using programs to monitor and automate their trades. They track their trades in spreadsheets and other software. They spend their days in front of a screen, communicating online with other traders all over the world. They interact with computers, not human beings, during the trading day. In fact, many successful day traders automate their trading — programming skills can be a big help.

Day traders are also self-employed, and many work from home. That means that if their software crashes, they have to fix it. They have to handle the upgrades, install the firewalls, and back up the data. Sure, you can pay someone to do these tasks, but the tech consultant probably won't be able to drop everything to get you up and trading again immediately. Hence, good day traders are comfortable with technology. If you like to mess around with programs, don't mind maintaining your computer, and understand how to set up your hardware for maximum efficiency, you're in good shape for day trading.

You don't have to be a self-employed day trader to trade securities. Brokerage firms, hedge funds, and exchange traders employ people to trade for them. In fact, most securities trading takes place through such larger organizations. But maybe you don't want to share your profits with someone else. Maybe you don't want someone dictating your strategy, placing limits on your trades, or determining your bonus based as much on factors such as teamwork and firm profitability as on what you brought in. You want to "eat what you kill," as they say, and day trading is one way you can do that.

When you day trade, you're responsible for your profits and your losses. That means that you reap the rewards and you don't have to share them with anyone else. It's a powerful incentive for independent people.

Good day traders have always been fascinated with the markets and how they move. If you watch CNBC for fun and have been following the securities business for years, no matter what your day jobs have been, then you may be a good candidate for day trading. Of course, I hope you've picked up more than "some people make a lot of money doing this!" A lengthy immersion in the cycles and systems that drive securities prices can help you develop trading strategies and know what you are up against.

And the markets are amazing, aren't they? All the buyers and sellers with all their different needs come together and find the price that gets the deal done. The prices assimilate all kinds of information about the state of the world, the desires of the people trading, and the future expectations for the economy. It's capitalism in its purest form, and watching how it works is almost magical. If you love how the markets work and want to learn first-hand what they tell you about making money, then by all means keep reading.

If you have never opened an account with a brokerage firm, purchased a stock, or invested in a mutual fund, you may not be suited for day trading. It's not that those activities alone are adequate preparation for day trading, but they're a start. They can help you understand all that can happen to cause you to make or lose money.

Much of the work of day trading takes place long before entering the buy or sell order. You have to define your trading system, see how it would have worked in the past, and test it to see how it works now. The preparatory work isn't as exciting as actually doing the day trading, because you aren't making real money, but you're not losing money, either.

Short-term trading has a huge potential for loss, and many traders are chasing the exact same ideas. The more you know about how your strategy works in different market conditions, the better prepared you will be to act appropriately and profitably.

It can take a long time to find a strategy that works enough of the time to make it worth your while. Many day traders spend months developing, testing, and refining their day trading strategy.

Because backtesting (which lets you test your trading strategy) uses historic prices, you can do much of the work on the side, at night, and on weekends, before you start day trading full time. It's a good way to get prepared for your trading business while you save your money and make other preparations for your new day trading venture.

Short-term traders don't have the luxury of thinking too much about what they're doing. Trading has to become intuitive. They have to be able to act on what they see when they see it. There's no room for second guessing, for hesitation, for choking, or for panic attacks.

Good day traders are also persistent. After they find a strategy they trust, they stick with it no matter how things are going. That's how they're able to buy low and sell high.

Even great traders go through bad periods, but if they trust their system and continue to stick with it, they usually pull out of the bad period, often with money ahead. If you've been able to stick it out when things went wrong other times in your life, you know what to expect when day trading.

Obviously, you want to make money. That's the whole idea of day trading. But day trading is difficult. Most traders quit in the first year. Some can't take the stress, some lose all their money, and some simply don't make enough money to make it worth their time.

Like any small business, you're taking a risk when you set up shop as a day trader. That risk is easier if you can afford to lose money. I'm not saying you need to have so much money that you won't miss it when it's gone, but you shouldn't be day trading with money you need to live on, any more than you would open a store or start a law practice with money you need to buy groceries and pay the mortgage.

If your household does not have a second source of income, be sure to set aside enough money to cover your living expenses while you get started. And you should keep a second pot of money, your walk-away fund, so that you're free to quit day trading and move on to your next adventure if you decide it's not for you.

It's especially important to have a financial cushion when you're day trading for the following reasons:

- You can afford to commit to your trading: Having your living expenses covered, at least at first, isn't just about dealing with losses. It's also about being able to stick with your trading. If you need cash to pay your bills, you may be tempted to take money out of the market whenever you're doing well. Doing so may keep you from reinvesting your profits. Plus, by not sticking to your strategy, your trading capital won't grow as fast. Think of day trading as a way to build a long-term asset, not a way to generate a steady stream of current income.

- You can stay in the market through the rough times: You know the old saying that the best way to make money is to buy low and sell high, right? Well, this means that the best time to buy is usually when securities prices have been beaten up and you've lost a lot of money. If you can afford some losses, staying in the game will be easier. Plus, you'll be able to stick to your strategy so that you can profit big when the market finally turns.

- You can better handle the stress of losses: Not all your trades are going to work out. Some days, you're going to lose money. If you have enough money that you don't fear loss, you can make better decisions. And you're less likely to panic if you know that you'll still be able to eat, pay your electric bill, and have a roof to sleep under at night. With sufficient funds, you're better able to view the markets clearly and follow a winning strategy.

Trading is very much a game of psychology. Give yourself an edge by waiting to do it until you can afford to.

Trading is stressful. The markets gyrate from events that no one can foresee. Things just happen, and no one else who's trading cares how these events affect you. It's enough to make you crazy some days, and unfortunately, some traders do get crazy. Alcoholism, depression, divorce, and suicide seem to be occupational hazards for those traders who have trouble separating what's happening in the market with who they are as people.

Chapter 1: What is Day Trading?

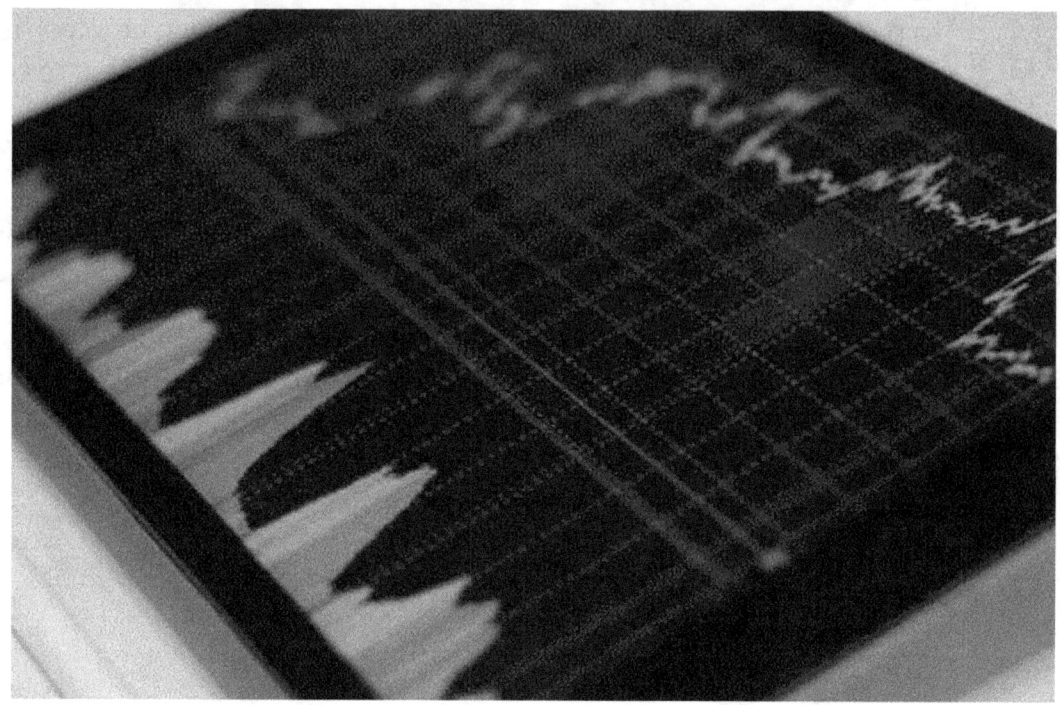

Day trading is the buying and selling of securities in one single trading day. This can occur in any type of marketplace that you choose but it is most common in the stock market and the forex market.

Day trading is a strategy of trading financial securities, such as stocks and currencies, where positions are taken and closed within the same day. Also called short trading, it involves buying a financial security and selling them before the trading day closes.

How short can day trading last? It can be as short as buying and selling in a few minutes, or even seconds! The point is to end the trading day with a square position, i.e., neither long nor short on any financial security.

Day trading can take place in any market, but the most common ones are the stock market and foreign exchange or forex markets.

When you start day trading, you'll need to start looking at financial securities from a different vantage point. For example, if you're used to swing trading or a buy-and-hold approach to stock market investing, you'll need to look at stocks differently when you day trade if you want to profit from it.

Instead of having a longer-term perspective on stocks, you'll need to reorient it to a very short-term one. In particular, you should shift your focus from a company's possible growth over the long term to its possible immediate price actions during the day.

Another area where you'll need to reorient your thinking are gains. Instead of looking at substantial gains, e.g., 10% or more, you'll need to scale down. Given the short time frame, you may have to make do with gains as low as 1% to 2%. This is because day trading involves trading at a higher frequency but with smaller gains, which accumulate over time.

You do not want to let your trade go on to the next day. This requires a different type of strategy than you will use with day trading. Mixing strategies during the same trade just to avoid a loss will make things worse. It is better to cut your losses with that trade and move on, closing out the trade before the end of the day.

With day trading, you are not going to make a ton of money off each trade. If you make a few dollars with each trade, you are doing a good job. The point here is to do a lot of small trades, taking advantage of the temporary ups and downs of the market. A lot of little profits can add up to a good payday when the process is done.

The potential profit that you can make from day traded is often misunderstood on Wall Street. Many internet scams like to take on this confusion and capitalize on it making a ton of money by promising significant returns in a short period. On the other side, the media continues to promote this trading method as a get rich quick scheme.

To determine whether you will be successful depends on a few essential factors. Mainly, if you jump into the day trading game without enough knowledge about the market and how this trading method works, you will probably fail. But many day traders can make a successful living from day trading. These individuals know about the market, have a good strategy in place, and can work with the market, despite the risks.

Day trading can be difficult. There are many professional financial advisors and money managers who worry about the risk of day trading and will shy away from it. They worry that in many cases, the reward is not going to justify all the risk that you take with day trading. It is possible to make a profit in this method but you have to know the market and you must have the time to fully watch the market at all times while completing your trade. Even those who do well in day trading will admit that the success rate with this method is often lower than the other methods of stock market trading.

Day trading isn't just restricted to stocks. You can day trade currencies, you can day trade commodities as well as options. Day trading involves more of a set of practices that you stick to.

Day trading is the very definition of short-term trading. It's all about the short term. Your trading horizon is restricted to one day. This means that you open a position and you close it strictly within one day's trading hours. You engage in its daily, you focus on one or more stocks or one or more commodities or currency pairings or options.

It's essential to keep in mind that all your positions are liquidated by the end of the day. Whether you make money or not, you are out of your position by the end of the day. That is the key definition of day trading.

How Day Trading Decisions Are Made

A day trader's decision whether to enter a stock or exit a stock all boils down to the probable movement of the pricing of the stock within the trading period. The trading period can be as short as 5 minutes or less or it can be the whole day. Whatever the case may be, it doesn't exceed the whole day.

Day traders make money off volatility. They do not make as much money when the stock is trading sideways for a long time and gradually slopes up. A stock might gain value 10% over a year, but that stock is off limits to a day trader because the volatility isn't there. They would instead trade a stock that bounces 15% up and down, every single day. That stock has enough inherent volatility on a day to day basis for day traders to make quite a bit of money.

What Benefit Do Day Traders Offer to the Market?

In terms of economic benefits, how does day trading benefit stock trading as a whole? Well, if anything, day traders provide liquidity to the stock market. They offer a ready base of buyers and sellers of stock. This provides the necessary movement of a stock's price that may encourage other traders to look at either the short term or long-term value and prospects of the stock. In other words, by providing action on a strictly short-term basis, day traders tend to shine a light on the overall attractiveness of a stock.

Keep in mind this is quite ironic because day traders, as a rule, do not look at the fundamentals of a stock. They don't look at the price/earnings ratio or P/E. They don't look at long term value, they don't look at industry positioning. They couldn't care less about any of that. Instead, they focus more on momentum, share movement, share volume and price velocity going either up or down.

How Day Trading Works

Once you start day trading, you can use an endless number of techniques and methods to execute trades. For example, you can choose to trade based solely on your "gut feeling" or you can go to the other extreme of relying entirely on mathematical models that optimize trading success through elaborate automated trading systems.

Regardless of the method, you can have limitless day-trading profit potential once you master day trading. Here are some of the strategies many expert day traders use profitably.

One is what's called "trading the news", which is one of the most popular day trading strategies since time immemorial. As you may have already gleaned from the name, it involves acting upon any press-released information such as economic data, interest rates, and corporate earnings.

Another popular day trading strategy is called "fading the gap at the open". This one's applicable on trading days when a security's price opens with a gap, i.e., below the previous day's lowest price or above the previous day's highest price.

"Fading the gap at the open" means taking an opposite position from the gap's direction. If the price opens with a downward gap, i.e., below the previous day's lowest price, you buy the security. If the price opens with an upward gap, i.e., it opens higher than the previous day's highest price, you short or sell the security.

There was a time when the only people able to trade in financial markets were those working for trading houses, brokerages, and financial institutions. The rise of the internet, however, made things easier for individual traders to get in on the action. Day Trading, in particular, can be a very profitable career, as long as one goes about it in the right way.

However, it can be quite challenging for new traders, especially those who lack a good strategy. Furthermore, even the most experienced day traders hit rough patches occasionally. As stated earlier, Day Trading is the purchase and sale of an asset within a single trading day. It can happen in any marketplace, but it is more common in the stock and forex markets.

Day traders use short-term trading strategies and a high level of leverage to take advantage of small price movements in highly liquid currencies or stocks. Experienced day traders have their finger on events that lead to short-term price movements, such as the news, corporate earnings, economic statistics, and interest rates, which are subject to market psychology and market expectations.

When the market exceeds or fails to meet those expectations, it causes unexpected, significant moves that can benefit attuned day traders. However, venturing into this line of business is not a decision prospective day trader should take lightly. Day traders can make a comfortable living trading for a few hours each day.

However, for new traders, this kind of success takes time. Think like several months or more than a year. For most day traders, the first year is quite tough. It is full of numerous wins and losses, which can stretch anyone's nerves to the limit. Therefore, a day trader's first realistic goal should be to hold on to his/her trading capital.

Volatility is the name of the game when it comes to Day Trading. Traders rely on a market or stock's fluctuations to make money. They prefer stocks that bounce around several times a day, but do not care about the reason for those price fluctuations. Day traders will also go for stocks with high liquidity, which will allow them to enter and exit positions without affecting the price of the stock.

Chapter 2: Basics Concepts of Day Trading

Day trading is characterized as the buy and offer of security inside a single trading day. It can happen in any marketplace; however, it is generally essential in the outside trade (forex) and financial exchanges. Day traders are commonly accomplished and very much subsidized. They utilize high measures of use and transient trading strategies to gain by little value developments in exceptionally liquid stocks or monetary standards.

Day traders are receptive to occasions that because momentary market moves. Trading the news is a well-known strategy. Planned declarations, for example, financial insights, corporate profit, or loan fees, are liable to market desires and market brain research. Markets respond when those desires are not met or are surpassed, as a rule with unexpected, noteworthy moves, which can profit day traders.

Day traders utilize various intraday strategies. These strategies include:

- Scalping, which endeavors to make various little benefits on little costs changes for the day

- Range trading, which fundamentally utilizes backing and obstruction levels to decide their purchase and sell choices

- News-based trading, which regularly holds onto trading openings from the increased volatility around news occasions

- High-recurrence trading (HFT) strategies that utilization refined calculations to misuse little or momentary market wasteful aspects

Remember that utilizing shorts, as clarified right now, not work for each trader. A few frameworks expect you to take each arrangement that goes along, regardless of whether you're up to or down, to exploit the edge that the framework gives.

Every trader has their degree of hazard resistance and wanted day by day, week after week, and month to month benefit targets. Numerous fruitful traders utilize every day, week by week, month to month, and even yearly shorts.

New traders shouldn't worry about benefit objectives; however, instead, center around consistency. That being stated, what are some practical benefit objectives for a fruitful Forex trader?

Setting Realistic Profit Targets in Trading

Everything begins with defining sensible day by day objectives. Swing traders may begin with week after week objectives for evident reasons. It is imperative to set your objectives in genuine benefits, instead of pips.

It is likewise imperative to utilize a similar measure of hazard (introduction) on each exchange. Fluctuating presentation is a decent method to clear out your record – regardless of whether you're utilizing a robust trading framework.

Day by day objectives is, to a great extent, controlled by your degree of hazard resistance. For example, you chance 1% per exchange. My day by day benefit cutoff is 2%, so you just need a couple of productive exchanges without any misfortunes to hit that mark.

If you are just gambling .5% per exchange, a progressively practical everyday benefit cutoff maybe 1% every day. It is going for 2%, while gambling .5%, would take two to four fruitful exchanges without any misfortunes to accomplish. It's not prone to occur.

Note: Don't simply hop into the market. Gain proficiency with a decent trading framework, and afterward back test and demo exchange until you demonstrate to yourself that you can be reliable over the long haul (months or years – not days or weeks).

At the point when you begin trading a live record, utilize the littlest part size (or the number of offers, contracts, and so forth...) accessible to you from the start. Step by step, increment your presentation per exchange to your ideal hazard level as you become acquainted with the mental obstacles of trading good money.

Best traders would prescribe utilizing .5 – 1% per exchange. Extremely propelled traders regularly hazard 3% or more per exchange. What amount of money would you say you will lose per exchange? When you have decided your degree of hazard resistance, you can decide a day by day objective or cutoff.

Week by week and Monthly Goals

From that point, your week after week and month to month shorts can be set. I have a progressively forceful hazard resilience, so I may benefit cutoff targets are as per the following: 2% every day, 5% week after week, and 15% month to month. I don't utilize yearly shorts.

These objectives may appear to be high to certain traders, yet they are sensible for me.

Note: This doesn't imply that you make 2% consistently, 5% consistently, and so on.... If you make 2% in a day, that is a decent day of trading. Moreover, 5% is a decent seven day stretch of trading.

If you are not reliable yet, you should concentrate on learning a beneficial trading framework and turning into a long haul, reliably productive trader. In case you're simply beginning, going for 5% every month bodes well.

If you feel that you can twofold your record at regular intervals in trading, you are not prone to set reasonable benefit targets. You will probably overtrade your way to a littler record balance.

You will chance excessively, and you will lose excessively. Ravenousness makes traders careless and overactive in the market, which prompts botches. Little predictable and exacerbated benefits will prompt a fortune over the long haul.

Keep in mind: Money management shorts work the two different ways. If you are down 2% in one day (or two misfortunes straight), Stop trading that day. Quit trading if you lose 3% in a multi-week. In conclusion, Use 5% as my month to month misfortunes cutoff. Remember that you will have a progressively forceful hazard resistance.

Advantages of Day Trading

If you need to trade stocks and hoping to turn into a day trader, it's critical to comprehend what you're getting yourself into and the advantages and the disadvantages. So, if you need to change and turn into a swing trader, at that point, you'll, in any event, know the purpose for it.

Most importantly, a day trader is somebody that holds stock or position, not exactly a day, which is 6 ½ hours, since the trading day last 6 ½ hours. So, you can hold it for 20 minutes, you can hold it for 60 minutes, you can hold it for five hours.

How about we talk about the advantages behind being a day trader. Bit of leeway number one is that a day trader has no medium-term hazard on holes or income since your hundred percent money before the day's over. The subsequent thing is that your income compound quicker, so in case you're bringing in money every day, you're ready to utilize the money that you produced using the earlier day to place into the following trading day.

It permits you to quicken your exacerbating income over and over truly. This is one of the extraordinary attractions to individuals for day trading is because it resembles brisk money. Presently additionally behind day trading, there's greater energy. This is regularly a passionate state, and a ton of beginner traders are truly pulled in today's trading since they find a workable pace account fluctuating here and there all over. Furthermore, you get sincerely attached to it; it resembles wow my benefit's going up. Or on the other hand, wow, this truly sucks, my benefits going down. There is that surge of the feelings that are going on yet again like I said that is ordinarily for fledgling or beginners, and it is anything but a decent method to be, in case you're hoping to exchange.

If effective, the prizes of day trading can far surpass the risks. Day trading requires order and time management. However, it additionally bears a person to make their hours without a chief or manager remaining over their back. What's more, notwithstanding the measure of money an individual can make structure the solace of their own home, day trading offers people numerous advantages they won't experience in the more customary types of trading stocks and other monetary instruments.

The key advantages of turning into a day trader:

Similar to any industry, there is a great deal of study and information to procure before plunking down before your PC and executing your first exchange. Be that as it may, an individual shouldn't be an expert in the fields of investing. There is a bounty of free assets on the Internet – and at your neighborhood library – that can help you bring your day trading profession. You can buy day trading programming (which can run you $20-30K) that can give you moment news, outlines, and stock data, however on the off chance that you are simply starting, this could be an error.

Numerous sites offer people the chance to rehearse and learn day trading on demo programming for nothing or a little charge (nobletraders.com; thousand years traders.com).

You work for yourself.

Simply envision: you are discreetly telecommuting on your PC, executing exchanges, tasting your espresso, yet something is feeling the loss of your chief or supervisor breathing down your neck. You work for yourself. You needn't bother with demand authorization for exchanges; you don't have to fulfill another person's need; you are in the game for yourself. You are dependable and responsible for your presentation. On the off chance that you fall flat, you lose money, conceivably an exceptionally huge sum. As much as we would all adoration this opportunity, it reminds you that you have to have the self-restraint and hard-working attitude to realize the business well.

Probably the best favorable position of day trading is the capacity to close your situation at or before the finish of the trading day. For a day trader who opens and closes his situation before the trading day closes, the risks of holding a stock medium-term are eradicated. A conventional trader's benefits can vanish medium-term with customary, long haul trading, however, with day trading, your benefits are verified as long as you close your situations before the finish of the trading day. This permits you – on the off chance that it was a decent day – to rest adequately around evening time.

No medium-term emergencies or cataclysms in the money related markets can influence your salary for that day.

Day traders can regularly exploit a battling market by using short-offering trading strategies to exploit falling stock costs. The capacity to bring in money off of the financial exchange in bear market conditions is a huge bit of leeway for a learned day trader.

There are two sorts of examination that most traders and investors look to for monetary data: technical investigation and key investigation. Customary, long haul traders have the chance to concentrate on an organization's essentials – organization wellbeing, fiscal reports, and management data – to perceive how its stock worth will change over the long haul.

Chapter 3: The Best Strategies

The thing to keep in mind is that the best strategy of a day trader is to find something that works and repeat it over and over again.

Once you have decided on that one strategy that works for you, placing and entry, setting a stop loss and taking a profit, then get on the simulator and practice! That's the way you will work out issues with your strategy. You can go over it as much as you want until you see continuous profit.

The goal is to be able to control your risk. You want to be able to control your trade risk and your daily risk.

- The amount you are willing to risk on each trade is referred to as your trade risk. That should ideally be equal to one percent or less of your capital on each trade. You can do that by selecting an entry point and then setting yourself a stop loss. The stop loss will get you out of the trade if the odds go too much against you. You should also learn how to calculate the position size for futures, stocks, and forex because knowing your position size will also help to keep your risk low.
- The amount that you lose in a day is your daily loss. It is smart to set a daily loss limit each day to avoid huge losses to yourself. If you have set your trade loss at one percent, you may want to set your daily risk at three percent. In that instance you would need to lose three or more trades with zero winners to lose three percent. And if you have practiced using your software and practiced using your strategy, that shouldn't happen often. You want to keep your daily loses small so that on winning days, they are easily recouped.

Trading only two or three hours per day is very common for day traders. However, some do trade for the whole session from nine thirty am until four pm, usually for the US stock market. All day traders are consistent in the hours they trade. They trade at the same hours each day whether they are trading for three hours or the whole session. Here are some of the hours you will want to focus on yourself:

- If you are going to be trading stocks, the best time of day for trading is the first hour and second hour right after the open, and the last hour of the day before the close. So, between 9:30am and 11:30am EST is the first two-hour period you want to find good trades. The biggest price moves and biggest profits are to be had at this time of day. Between 3:00pm and 4:00pm EST is a good hour of the day also. There are pretty big moves then also, however, if you are going to only trade for two hours in a day, trade in the morning. That's when the market is the most volatile.

- If you will be trading futures, the opening time is the better time to trade. That would be between 8:30 am and 11:00 am EST. Active futures see activity around the clock, so the best trading times are a little earlier then with stocks. Futures markets officially close at different times and the last hour of a contract can also offer sizable moves for you to get in on.
- If you decide to trade the forex market, they trade twenty-four hours a day during the week. The EURUSD is the favorite of the day traders. It is the most volatile between 0600 and 1700 GMT. These are the hours when the day traders should trade this market. The biggest price moves are between 1200 and 1500 GMT. This is when both the US and London markets are open, trading the euro and US dollar.

We mentioned before that day traders find a strategy and then repeat it over and over again. That is what we will talk about now in more detail. These are the basic day trading strategies that are used. There are many others, but these are the most common.

Scalping: Probably the most common of the strategies is scalping. It is a basic get in there and get out of there type of mind frame toward trading. Day traders will get in on a good trade and then sell as soon as it starts to show profitability. It's relatively safe and that's why a lot of people like it. You don't watch it and then hope it stays strong.

Daily Pivots: A day trader using this strategy would look to buy their trade at its lowest price during the day and then try to sell it at its highest price of the day. These times are also referred to as low of the day (LOD) and high of the day (HOD).

Fading: This is known as a risky strategy. Day traders will short stocks once they start to gain rapidly. The theory being that the stocks are over purchased and the traders who purchased early will be looking to sell because the stock is gaining and they are making money. The other traders may be scalping. This strategy of fading can be profitable when used correctly, but keep in mind that the risk is higher.

Momentum: If you are a person who would be interested in riding trends, then this type of trading may be a perfect strategy for you. The day traders who enjoy this method watch the current news and are watching for the trends being supported by the highest volumes of trades. Then they jump on the wagon and ride the waves until they see signs of it turning around. Then of course they are watching the news releases and they just start all over again.

Stop Losses: The use of stop losses is crucial in day trading. The market is so prone to sharp price movements and you could potentially see substantial losses in a short amount of time if you aren't careful. There are two types of stop losses which we covered earlier. The physical stop loss order and the mental stop loss. During your whole day trading career, you need to keep these stop losses in the front of your mind.

These strategies that I have given you are not miracle strategies. Just because you master one, it won't make you rich. The main secret lies in consistency. Always be looking at your strategies and evaluating them. Tweak them to work for you by adding other parts of other strategies to them. Use them to find your comfort zone. Find what works for you. It has taken many of the most elite day traders' years to hone and perfect their unique strategies.

If you are to be a successful day trader, aside from reading this book, you must have patience. You may wait minutes to days for a profitable trade to come along. You must be able to make smart decisions. Knowing when to get in and out of a trade is vital. There could be a profitable situation staring you in the face and you have maybe minutes to react. And of course, you must be able to maintain balance. How you react to winning and losing is so important. One day, you can be on cloud nine because the day went perfectly. The next day you could be down in the dumps and depressed because you may have taken a nasty loss. You must maintain balance there for your emotional wellbeing.

Chapter 4: Rules for Successful Day Trading

When a trader gets into trading, they are very hopeful that everything will play out well and that in no time, they will start making a lot of profits. To succeed in trading, a trader must know what trade is all about. This means that they should fully be aware of the strategies in trading, risks involved, and how to manage the risks, and also importantly, understand the psychology involved in the trade.

Understand Your Motive

It is essential to understand what you are about to put yourself through. Understand why you want to venture into trading, is it because you want to make money or because others are doing it? Knowing your primary motive for joining trading will save you from losing money. Trading involves you invest your money into the investment. Therefore, before you invest your money, it's good to learn all that trading entails. Without understanding the market, you are likely to lose money in ways you would have avoided had you first taken some lessons. Trading sounds so easy to someone who has not gotten into it, but along the way, they find out that it was not as easy as it seemed. Therefore, for a beginner trader, it is essential that they fully understand the business before investing in large sums of money. It is vital that as a trader, you understand how to stick to your methods no matter how tempting it gets. Sticking to your strategy shows that you trust your understanding of the market and cannot easily quit.

Never Stop Learning

For a trader, there's never enough knowledge of the market. The trading patterns keep changing; you need to keep learning why the changes are taking place. You also need to know what to do with the changes and what strategies will work. Learning the basics and understanding the trading market is essential, but a trader has to be more open to learning every time. For a successful trader long-term trader, they have to keep up with new technologies that may affect the market. This means keeping up with the world's happenings as that is what will affect the trade market.

Realize Your Goal

Understand your trading goals, as this will help you push on when the market doesn't seem to be working out well for you. The primary purpose of trading is to get money, but you should have a reason for why you need the money. Having the exact reason in your mind why you need the money will keep you more motivated to be a better trader every day. A clear objective will make you want to keep going even when you feel like giving up.

Identify Your Flaws as Well as Your Strengths

Immediately you start trading. You must identify your weaknesses. The earlier you learn about your shortcomings, the quicker you get to work on it before you are exposed to losing money. You will get to know if the weaknesses are something you could work on by yourself, or you will need help from other experienced traders. It is good, however, to try working by yourself first since then, that means that you get to learn your weaknesses further. When this doesn't work out, then it is good to seek help from other traders. Identifying your strength is essential as it will help you stop wasting time when you can follow your strengths to achieve an intended trade goal. This will also help you schedule your time well so that you can balance your weaknesses and strengths. Every trader is different; what one trader finds to be their weakness could be another trader's strength and vice versa. The trick is to identify what will do for you as a trader. The trader, therefore, has to find out where they are going wrong and amend or replace the mistakes for better trading experiences.

Allow Yourself Time

Traders get into the market with so many expectations about the market. They imagine that they will enter the market, put some money and the next minute they are swimming in millions of moneys. Trading is profitable when done right, but it also needs time before you finally enjoy your benefits. Allow yourself time to adapt to the market, to know how trading works, and even understand the many risks you are likely to incur. Allowing yourself time to just adjust to the market without so much greed for the money will make you a very great trader who will succeed in the long run. It is better to make small profits for a long time than to make huge profits for a short while. Not being ready is essential for a trader; it will give him the patience to wait and work towards being great traders rather than just focusing on being short term traders. It will also make the trader love their trading experiences because they are not rushing themselves or putting too much unnecessary pressure on themselves.

Have a Network of Fellow Traders?

Like all other businesses, traders are supposed to create friendships among themselves. These fellow traders will not only inspire a trader, but they will offer help to the trader when the trader needs it. It is good to have friends doing the same thing as you are as you get to hear their experiences, and you can compare them with your own experiences. Having friends who been in trading longer than you have will give awareness of what awaits you in the long run. You can get some things to copy from a friend who has been doing this ahead of you. Having friends who are in the same industry will also give you a friend counselor or mentor who will help you in making various trade decisions. You can make this advisor your mentor whom you will consult from time to time. A mentor will help you avoid making bad trading decisions that could cost you a lot of money and also help you identify how to work out your weaknesses. A network is generally crucial because even other than having people who will offer you help; you also have people who can give you future connections in the market.

Love the Trading Market

To love the trading experience means that you enjoy the process more than your love for the money that comes along. By doing this, it means that even when you don't get so much money from the process, you will push on with the trade because you love the thrill of trading. The benefits are vital without them; there would be no reason to do trading. However, the benefits will not be very rewarding for someone who does not enjoy the process of getting them. This is even more so because you may lose all the money you had invested in trading, but if you love the process, you will know how to pick yourself back up. The rewards are not very fulfilling for a trader if the trader does not enjoy his journey and keeps waking up to make the trade just for the money. Enjoying the process gives you reasons to take more risks that will yield you more profits. But when you do not enjoy the process, you only play safely to maintain the same earnings as you make every day. If you can maintain a standard point, you do not care for anything else. Loving the process means that you get to explore more to understand the market and also to find ways that will make you enjoy your work more. When you love trading, you are not like to be as exhausted when working as people who do not enjoy it. When you enjoy the trading process, you are likely to adjust to the market quickly and even succeed more than traders who have been doing it for long.

Stick to What You Know

The trading market is diverse, stick to what you are comfortable in rather than wasting your time going for different strategies. It is good to be open to new methods, but if the ways just spend your time or slow your progress, it is good to stick with what you know. Take time to modify what you have because that may be more beneficial for you as a trader. The art of mastering the industry involves that you deal with the little you know and work on it until perfection. When you have perfected one area, you can then pick another area and work on it. In short, it is good to subdivide your trading schedules and work on them individually than picking a big task that will not yield you much results.

Keep Practicing

It is good for a trader to first try by practicing to ensure that they are more comfortable in the market before investing their money. Practicing before you finally get to put your money will give you security because you already know what you are about to face. You may achieve this by using a trading simulator, which will help you get a feel of the real work awaiting you. When you finally are convinced that you are up to the task, then you can venture into trading. Then when you eventually become a trader, it is good to keep putting into practice all the different methods you learn along the way. Every opportunity as a trader should be used to perfect on your skills, and the way to perfecting is by ensuring that you are not lazy but keep learning.

Don't Be Too Excited

Excitement is good, but in trading, it will cost you a lot. You may be too excited and end up making rushed decisions that will make you losses. Sometimes the market works too much in your favor that you begin to think you are perfect. You may keep getting it right, but you still need to be careful because getting too excited may make you make a small mistake that will bring you down. Your strategy may be working, but that does not make you an overnight prophet that you now think your predictions are always right. You will still need to keep observing the market; you will still need to keep trying different strategies because there is no guarantee that you will keep winning. Losing several times, on the other hand, does not make you a definite failure. You don't have to keep taking bigger risks to ensure that you recover your money. Take your time and strategize your moves and see where you are going wrong instead of crucifying yourself. Do not be too hard on yourself simply because a few times. The plan didn't work out for you. But also, do not let the excitement make you too overconfident as overconfident is most likely to bring you down. When you can seem to strike a balance, it is good to take a break from trading and relax. Continuing like this will be more harmful to you than if you had relaxed.

Chapter 5: Day Trading vs. Swing Trading

Most companies in the financial markets are familiar with the different schedules that traders might have in the day to day lives; therefore, they made a consideration. All stocks in the market are categorized according to their traders.

Traders are grouped into two categories:

- swing traders
- day traders

Swing Traders are those who buy stocks that are not fast perishable and therefore stay on the market longer.

Day Traders are in the market for something fast-moving and has a high volatility rate.

This distinction makes the different types of trading applicable to those in the market. How to identify what stocks are suitable for day trading or swing trading is reliant on the information gotten from the different platforms.

Different website platforms are perfect for this dissemination of information as they are regularly updated and get direct information from those companies and big investors.

There is also a stark financial difference between day trading and swing trading, and all these niches are analyzed in this chapter.

Read on.

Day trading vs swing trading

Just when you thought you were getting a grip on day trading; you discover that there is another type of trading. Swing trading is another form of trading that is undertaken by people who have not as much time as the day traders.

Similarities

While there are more stark contrasts, there are also a few similarities between these two modes:

- Day trading and swing trading are easily tracked and charted regularly. Their activity on the market is manageable, and statistics well documented regularly.
- There is always a possibility for huge profits based on the stockiest on the market. When the stockist's graph has been on a constant rise, both day and swing traders are bound to reap heavily from it.
- There is no limit to the number of stocks. However, you will need to stick to the max dollar stop-loss rule. Both types of trading allow for the purchase of the viable stocks, and this is essential as they use different time frames to track.

- Both of these types of trading can be done on the same platforms, and the transactions remain the same.
- There is a real-time opportunity to keep track of the charting of your stock performance at will in both day and swing trading. There are the limit and timer that can be set by the trader to go off at the time of analysis.

Differences

All traders are grouped into two categories: swing traders and day traders.

- Day trading is for people who are impulsive and have a high level of discipline. Swing traders tend to be more cautious and take a long-time making decision hence the amount of time they use.
- Day trading is based mostly on making profits unlike swing trading that is done so as to identify swings in stocks and occurrences in the forex market over a period of time.
- When it comes to risks, day trading carries the most. Day traders, therefore, have to invest a lot of time in the markets due to the longevity of their stocks. Swing trading only carries the risk of having the amount out on the market for long.
- Day trading can be drawn back with a power outage while swing trading will carry on even after the power is back. Therefore, one should constantly have backup internet access or an alternative form of communication on their stocks.
- Day trading is full time while swing trading doesn't have to be.
- Day trading rarely works with high-value stocks and focuses more on small and retail companies while swing trading mostly stocks belonging to corporate companies.
- A swing trader is able to concentrate on his own personal off time and probably strengthen his trading skills as opposed to a day trader. The day trader is always rushing to make as much profit from the maximum number of stocks he purchased to hone his skills.
- Day trading involves more bank transactions than swing trading. This is because, in the buying of stocks, the bank is involved whereas swing traders do that less often. This is likely to increase the day traders' chances at daily transactions than that of a swing trader.
- Day trading involves more charting of stocks and thus a better understanding of fast-moving stocks than swing traders.

- Swing traders stand to lose out in case of a market crash than day traders are they are done with everything at the end of the day. This takes a lot of faith in that their stocks will payout and not burn out.

Swing trading comes with different opportunities and also frequent scares. These trades are made in shaky markets, and any time the market can crash with all those dollars invested in it.

Swing trading is also best experienced once one has mastered the art of money management so that you can project your profits wisely. This advanced time on the market will help you identify the patterns in the stocks, and this will improve your decision-making ability. In any business investment, the management of money matters a lot. We have had some businesses start out really well and ended up failing. You will be amused that they do not fail due to the lack of a good strategy. Instead, they fail due to poor management of finances. Any business that looks forward to making more profits, as the years advance, needs to look at how they manage their finances keenly. We have heard of cases where businesses started out well only to end up failing before making bigger strides. Money laundering has affected many businesses to the point of closure. Once you know how to engage in swing trading, ensure that you manage your finances. This will ensure that you make better decisions while carrying out various trades. With a good money management strategy, it gets easier to make progress in swing trading. You find that you will easily double your profits with this strategy.

Due to the longer time frames, have a reliable mode of communication as one is bound to forget to make moves on the market, thus ending up with huge losses. Timing is important in all the business deals that you engage in. The interesting thing about most motivational talks is how they insist on proper time management. You have probably come across some people that would prefer you to waste their money but not their time. The importance of time lies in the impact that it has on an individual. The time factor is also necessary while conducting various trades. Ensure that you are keen on the decisions that you make.

For instance, with the long durations in which the trades are carried out, you may forget the time you were required to trade. You find that you have a lot going on and keeping certain dates becomes a challenge. To avoid this, you can set a reminder on when you need to trade. At times, this will require that you are disciplined in carrying out your various activities. The decisions that you make, no matter how small, hold a big impact in your possibility of succeeding. Utilizing this strategy will help you a lot while trading options. It ensures that you are disciplined in keeping time and you trade in moments when you can get a big profit.

Observe the trends in the market and steer clear of trading with the trend. This is because its longevity might be questionable and therefore having a stock that phased out while you were not tracking it is detrimental. Avoid trading against the most appealing trend and exercise caution by withholding yourself. As a trader, you need to be keen on how the market moves. You cannot achieve success in a certain area unless you fully understand what it entails. As an individual intending to engage in swing trading, one of the best strategies that you can utilize is knowing how the market operates. You will be surprised by the power of having information. In the world that we currently live in, ignorance will cost you a lot. Nowadays, information is readily available to us that one has no excuse not to learn.

Be mentally prepared to make losses as much as you are prepared to make profits. This is an inevitable step in the trading process. Day trading is unpredictable as a stock can crash at any time during the day. This strategy has been a challenge for most people. You find that you are not open to the possibility of incurring a loss. Asides from the fact that the main purpose of investing is earning a profit, you have to be open to the challenges that come with investments. At times trades go contrary to what we expected. A single mistake can cause you to encounter a loss. At times, we have no control over some factors, and once we encounter a loss. While you engage in day trading, know that you can either win or lose at the end of the day. This will protect you from stress and other challenges that result from being stressed. You get to appreciate your efforts despite failing since you understand that failure is part of the success journey. Not every person can do this, but we need to encourage ourselves.

The time invested must be more than any other investment. The individual must set aside enough time to track and chart the stocks in order to see their performance and enable him to exit at the opportune time.

Use the percent rule in terms of funds. You must be willing to lose a bit so as to gain a lot in the financial markets. Some stocks are liable to burn while others are clear wins. At times we are advised that we need to part with money to make money. As we aspire to get rich, there are some major decisions that we will need to make. At times it will involve making sacrifices to get to the levels and positions that we aspire to be in. the path to success is not an easy journey, but we have to be fully committed to the process.

Avoid being enticed by buying so many stocks at once. Start small and get a maximum of two stocks that are easily managed within the small-time frame that day trading provides. You are also likely to get more opportunities with these few stocks on the market. At times we have a misguided belief that the more stock one has, the more money they are likely to have. Contrary to this belief, one can make a loss while using such a strategy. Buying multiple stocks results in overtrading, and you may end up having overleveraged accounts. As a beginner, start with manageable stocks that you can handle. This allows you to evaluate the various stocks before purchasing them easily. You get to know the stocks that can earn you a profit as you avoid the stocks that will not help you in generating an income. Some expert traders are also unable to conduct multiple trades since they know the challenges that come with trading. This should show you how risky it is and help you avoid engaging in such. Ensure that you only engage in trades that you can manage so that you make wise decisions.

Chapter 6: Financial Instrumental for Swing Trading

In general, more profits mean more income. We for the most part imagine that others should pay us more in the event that we need to get more cash-flow. In any case, this isn't in every case valid: we can acquire all the more regardless of whether we pay ourselves more, and not the others.

This is a key guideline hidden the budgetary achievement, first revealed in 1926 by George Samuel Clason through his book entitled The Richest Man in Babylon, an incredible persuasive exemplary.

The standard expresses that piece of what you win must be kept up. Setting aside in any event 10% of what you procure - and bringing in that cash difficult to reach to standard costs and conceivably even exceptional costs - you can build this sum exponentially after some time. Thinking about any ventures, on account of the intensity of the compound speculation, the sum spared/contributed - throughout the years - can get significant. Numerous individuals can procure more and construct their benefits by paying themselves first. Today is a valid and successful rule as it was in 1926.

However, as this 10% equation is simple, individuals are reluctant to hear it out and apply it. This is on the grounds that you are normally searching for stunts to get rich rapidly, and you don't have a medium to long haul vision. Then again, having a drawn-out venture plan is a strong establishment on which to assemble one's monetary strength. Also, you can begin acquiring more by paying yourself first from today. The prior you start and the speedier you will construct your money related achievement.

Compound Interest: Using its power

To gain more, you can exploit the compound interest. Here's the means by which it works: on the off chance that you contribute 1,000 dollars at a 5% premium, you will procure 50 dollars of premium, and toward the finish of the principal year, you will have an all-out speculation of 1,050 dollars. In the event that you leave both the underlying speculation and the premium earned on the present record, you will get a 5% premium the next year over $ 1,050, or $ 52.50. In the third year, you will acquire 5% out of 1.102.50, etc. Because of current circumstances, inside 15-30 years, your cash will transform into a sum well over the entirety contributed at first. However, unequivocally what amount does the contributed capital develop? The Italian mathematician Luca Pacioli clarified it in the fifteenth century: any capital copies in a total of 'years' equivalent to 72 which you will partition by the 'loan fee.' Returning to our model: if the intrigue is at 5% every year, we isolate 72 by 5; which makes 14.4, i.e., in 14 years and four months the underlying capital duplicates. The sooner you start and the greater the outcome will be, as you will possess more energy for the intrigue you exploit delivering its amazing enchantment. Start currently to spare and contribute for your future, regardless of whether you don't have an enormous entirety. You don't have to have an additional entirety of cash. You can begin with any sum and develop it after some time.

The secret of paying of yourself first

In the event that you need to acquire more cash by 'paying yourself first,' you need to make reserve funds and speculation a focal piece of your money related administration, much the same as the home loan installment. Get familiar with sparing a fixed rate (in any event 10%) of your month to month pay and putting it in uncommon investment account that you choose not to contact. In a perfect world, this progression would be programmed, for example, a fixed month to month finding on your check. The computerization will guarantee that you won't need to depend on your self-restraint, and your capacity to spare won't be influenced by your state of mind, from household crises or something else. Keep on expanding that account until you have spared enough to put the entirety aggregated in securities, in a shared store or land (burning through cash on lease without building any benefits is a waste). Let your speculations construct your advantages after some time, and attempt to live with what stays after you have paid yourself. If you need to spend, attempt to gain more to bear the cost of it. Be that as it may, never put your hands on your investment funds to back a progressively eager way of life. The perfect would be for your ventures to develop to where you could live with intrigue, if essential. At exactly that point will you be monetarily self-governing and free.

If you need to gain more, you have to make resources, not liabilities. As opposed to going through all the cash you gain, by enhancing another person, put resources into resources that produce other pay (stocks, bonds, land, gold, and so forth.). At that point when your cash begins to develop, instruct yourself further about the most ideal approach to put away your cash. Remain educated about news about venture openings and make sure to secure what is yours through a decent protection approach. Don't aimlessly believe who will deal with your cash, yet consistently attempt to improve your monetary instruction. This will make you a monetarily arranged individual, prepared to get rich. When you get this, the cash will follow.

What is accruing funds? Not every person may realize how to react quickly to this inquiry. Truth be told, if everybody recognizes what the basic intrigue is, i.e., the one that pulls back toward the finish of the concurred time unit, less are the individuals who comprehend what the accumulating funds is, the means by which it works and, above all, how to exploit it.

The case of a ledger is edifying.

On the off chance that on 1 January I have a net pace of 1% for me, toward the year's end I have 101 euros. The euro more is added to the capital and, if the conditions don't change, toward the finish of the second year I won't have 102 euros, however 102 euros and 1 penny where the penny speaks to 1% of the euro collected after the primary year.

Up until this point, everything is clear, yet a large portion of us can't compute the accruing funds of speculation and will in general treat it as straightforward intrigue. This is because of its moderate beginning, that, particularly with little capital, will in general be treated as "immaterial." However, there is nothing increasingly wrong that a financial specialist could do.

In the event that, for instance, following five years of speculation, my capital of 100 euros is currently 140, we are persuaded that the intrigue was 8% every year.

This is mistaken in light of the fact that, in doing as such, we don't consider that toward the finish of every period, the intrigue aggregate has gone to build capital. In the event that the intrigue had been 8%, creating the five years, we would have had

Introductory capital: 100

- 1st year: 108
- 2nd year: 116.64
- 3rd year: 125.97
- 4th year: 136.04
- 5th year: 146.93

The distinction (6.93 euros) speaks to nearly 7% of the aggregate. From the model, it clear to take astonish (and more regrettable, even "endure," if for reasons unknown we are offered a basic enthusiasm for accruing funds).

The math behind compound interest: an easy example

Assume we have an underlying capital of 1,000 euros. The capital yields a Y% intrigue and this intrigue is determined on a yearly premise.

The figuring recipe is as per the following:

(1) $IV = CP (1 + Y)^X$

IV is the estimation of the speculation after X years, while CP is the underlying capital. Y is communicated as a rate, i.e., 0.04 shows 4%. The image $\wedge$ is the image of rise to control.

The converse count will in general discover the Y enthusiasm of a venture that currently (net of expansion) is worth IV against a CP capital contributed X periods (years) prior. The equation is:

(2) $Y = (IV/CP)^{(1/X)} - 1$

Assume that, after expansion, 1,000 euros contributed five years back are currently worth 1,400 euros, you promptly have that the yield was 6.96%.

How about we investigate another model

Marie has quite recently taken the compensation and can at last purchase the forced air system she needs

In any case, her companion Julie calls her to reveal to her that she has a critical need that she can't adapt to promptly and requests that her obtain $ 1,000.

Marie is uncertain on the grounds that this would mean holding up one more month before she can make her buy.

To determine the issue, the two young ladies concede to the advance gave that Julie restores the cash to Mary with a 5% premium (the numbers are absolutely arbitrary for the model).

Right now, Marie has a more noteworthy motivator to need to postpone her buy.

When Julie restores the aggregate advanced, she will get $ 1,050 rather than $ 1,000.

The next month Marie would then be able to purchase the forced air system and, to commend, utilize the $ 50 interest to go out to supper with her beau.

To put it plainly, at last, this acknowledgment for the postponed utilize was not terrible!

Since we comprehend the idea driving the pace of interest, it is a great idea to enter somewhat more in detail and make a few qualifications.

Right now, can partition the loan fee into two general classes:

- The simple interest;
- The compound interests.

Simple Interest

Toward the finish of the period, Julie restores the cash in addition to the interest to Mary. Before long, be that as it may, the young lady asks a similar sum again to purchase another cooler, as the bygone one abruptly broke.

Marie consents to loan the cash back to her companion.

The next month Julie solidified her obligation in addition to new interests, again for a sum of $ 1,050.

Presently Marie is with her underlying capital, in addition to $ 100 in interest, for an aggregate of $ 1,100.

Interest is characterized as basic when, when it has developed on the fundamental capital, it doesn't create further interest.

In our model, we note that the initial 50 $ were not added to the capital credited the subsequent time.

Compound Interest

Change of scenery.

Julie asks Marie to loan her $ 1,000 with the guarantee to return them in two years.

Mary concurs, as long as Julie acknowledges a self-multiplying dividend on the develop acquired capital.

Right now, won't need to pay the interest quickly toward the finish of the first year yet will include the $ 50 interest for the capital, which thusly will aggregate 5% in the second year.

Toward the finish of the concurred period, Julie should in this way return:

o$ 1,000 capital

o$ 50 interest for the principal year ($ 1,000 + 5%)

o$ 52.50 interest for the second year ($ 1.050 + 5%)

The all-out cash-flow to be come back to Mary is, along these lines, $ 1,102.50.

Here we have emerged $ 2.50 more than the past model, because of the accruing funds.

Chapter 7: Swing Trading Guiding Principles

Before I discuss various strategies that can be used to swing trade, let's look at the basic guiding principles that I build these strategies on. They are as follows:

1. Keep it simple.
2. Treat your swing trading activity like a serious business.
3. Develop a work plan and stick with it.
4. Actively manage your risk to reward ratio; focus on the entry.
5. Measure your results and adjust accordingly.

Each of these principles is discussed in more detail below.

Keep it Simple

You may have heard of the term "paralysis by analysis". This happens when you analyze something to the point where you cannot make a decision. Some swing traders overcomplicate their analysis of a security by using multiple indicators that all have to line up for them to enter a trade. In real life, everything does not often line up perfectly and you have to go with what you feel is right.

I have thus far covered many different tools and indicators you can use to help you to make a decision. You do not need to use all of them to be a successful swing trader. Once you find 1 or 2 that work well for you, you should then stick with those. If you decide to use a few different tools that all need to align, it will likely mean that you are not going to be trading very often. That is not necessarily a bad thing though. It is better to sit on your hands and wait for a good trade versus jumping in and out of marginal trade setups and slowly lose your money. The only one who wins in that case is your broker, as they collect fees for all of your trades (the successful ones and the losing one's).

Find several indicators that work well for you and focus on using them. Don't trade often, but trade smart, by knowing why you are entering a trade and, most importantly, knowing your risk to reward ratio and exit price points. As you gain more experience in swing trading, you will be able to recognize better trades that are going to work out even if everything is not perfectly aligned.

Having said this, when you do happen to find a number of indicators that are all aligned with the trade you are considering taking, it can certainly provide some level of confidence that you have a potentially profitable trade.

Treat your Swing Trading Activity Like a Serious Business

Should you decide that swing trading is a right fit for your personality, and that it is able to fit into your life along with all of your other interests and responsibilities, then you need to treat this activity as a very serious business. It will require an investment of time and effort, which hopefully will lead to some very good rewards.

Have a designated area where you do your research and keep all of your records. You are essentially becoming a professional money manager for yourself, so you should keep your work organized at all times. Everything you do with your business should be oriented toward making sure you are a success. If you feel like a professional, then you are more apt to trade like one.

Develop a Work Plan

Have a work plan and stick with it. Your work plan should include checking the market at the open and before the close. During this time, you should monitor your positions, set alerts and possibly enter orders at target levels that you think might get filled during the trading day.

I also recommend that you review your portfolio and market performance every night from Sunday to Thursday to ensure your assumptions about your positions and portfolio are still valid. On the weekend, you should try to do a more thorough review.

It is important to establish a work plan and keep it consistent. By keeping your work plan relatively consistent, you can measure your performance without introducing additional variables. Measuring your performance allows you to find areas to improve and make changes as you see fit.

I will discuss the routine of a swing trader in Chapter 14, which you can adopt or use as a guide to developing your own plan that works for you and your specific situation.

Actively Manage your Risk to Reward Ratio; Focus on the Entry

As a swing trader, your first and most important tool is your capital or cash. As I have said before, without cash you cannot be a trader. I have written at length already about the necessity of assessing the risk to reward ratio on every trade and also on how much capital you should put into each trade. Following your rules on these points will prevent you from quickly losing all of your capital. You will be wrong on your trades some of the time and you need to make sure you live to trade another day.

Just planning and knowing your stop-loss and profitable exits are not enough for swing trading. Your entry becomes the next important step in your trade. You have already determined your stop-loss point and your target price(s) for a profitable exit. However, you calculated the risk to reward ratio based on an assumed entry price point.

Let's assume you found a good setup during a scan in the evening after the market has closed. The security closed the day at $10.50 and you see an upside to $12.00 with support at $10.00 where you would stop out. Therefore, you have a potential $0.50 loss compared to a $1.50 gain to the upside. That is a 1 to 3 risk to reward ratio, which is very good, and you are ready to pull the trigger and place a buy order in the morning. The market opens the next morning and the security you are ready to buy opens up at $11.00. What do you do? The novice trader is already invested mentally in the trade so they buy. Unfortunately for them, their risk to reward is now 1 to 1 with the downside to $10.00 and upside to $12.00. This is no longer a good trade at that entry point.

The rational trader reassesses the situation. They may put a buy order in at $10.50, hoping to catch the entry they wanted on the security during the normal daily price gyrations in the market. This will give them the risk to reward ratio that they need to make a good swing trade. If they do not get a fill, then they need to reassess again, and maybe move on to finding another trade with a more appropriate risk to reward ratio.

The bottom line, do not get emotional and chase a trade. The "fear of missing out" can motivate you to make a bad trade and you should be aware of this when picking your entry price on a trade.

Measure your Results and Adjust Accordingly

As a trader, you must track your results to measure your performance. Nothing gets improved that does not get measured first. Every trader should use a tool to record the different aspects of each trade, from initial assessment through to the risk to reward expected, the entry point, and, finally, the exit. The tool can be a spreadsheet, it can be done on paper or it can be web-based. It does not matter how you do it as long as the process allows you to track the details of each trade as well as your performance.

Once you have your trades recorded in detail, you can go back at any time and review how the trade worked. You can compare your performance on using the different indicators, i.e., is one working particularly well versus the others that you use? Are you getting good entry points on your trades or do you need to exercise more patience? Are your exits working or are you consistently exiting a trade too early and not getting all of the money you could on a profitable trade? Are you respecting your stops?

Having all of this information to review will help you adjust your trading process and plan accordingly to maximize your performance without letting emotion enter into your decision-making. I will discuss the details of using a journal to track your trades in Chapter 14, Routines of a Swing Trader.

Chapter 8: Swing Trading Strategies

Now that we have had a lot of time to look at what swing trading is all about and how great it can be to work with this method of investing, it is time to take this a little bit further and look more at some of the strategies that we can use to really take our swing trading and make it as effective as possible. These strategies can all work in certain types of trades, and it depends on what you are the most comfortable with and how the market is behaving. Learning at least a few of them and gaining some confidence when using them will make a world of difference in how well you can make this happen. Let's dive in and look at some of the best options that you can go with when it is time to start swing trading

The ABCD Pattern

Another option that is really nice if you are into swing trading as a beginner is the ABCD pattern. This one is going to start us off with an upward move that is really strong. When this happens, you have a lot of buyers who are aggressively purchasing stock from point A, and then they will constantly bring in some new highs for that day, which will be point B. it is important to try and get in at B and trade here. But you do not want to chase the trade at all because B is usually higher than what the price is in the first place. Plus, this point is at a part where it is hard to know where to place the stop loss, and you do not want to get into a trade without this.

When you see that Point B shows up, the traders who have already gone in and purchased the stock at point A that we talked about earlier, will then start to sell off their stocks. This will not all happen at once, but it will slowly happen as a few decide to take the profits and call it good. This is not the time where you should enter the trade because it is hard to know when and where that pullback is going to happen.

If you are able to see that there is a bottom to this and the price just doesn't seem to go any further than it, then this is your point C. The security has found its support level, and you can go in and start planning the trade that you would like to use. If you get in at the right time and plan all of this out well, then you should be able to make a good amount of profit in the process.

This is a simple strategy that we are able to work with, which is why we are introducing it to you as a beginner. It is easy to understand and follow, and you won't feel as lost and confused along the way as some others may when they work on this one. There are a number of steps that we will have to use when we want to see this one work, and some of the steps will include:

- When you take a look through the scanner that you have set up, and you are looking for a stock, you want to look for one that is going to surge up from its original point A. You want it to get to a new high for that day. This is going to be point B.

- When these forms, you need to start paying attention. If you see that the new price is then going to become the support, and it goes up even more from there, then that is going to be point C. Be careful when you take a look at this because you have to wait for the right signs, rather than making assumptions and entering the market too soon.

- After you see the Point C showing up, you need to watch the stock carefully through this kind of consolidation period. From the information that you are able to gather at this time, you can then choose the right share size that you are comfortable with trading. You also need to spend this time looking for the stop and exit strategy that you would like to work with.

- When you see that the price is holding onto that support at point C, you should enter a trade at a point that is on or close to point C. The goal here is that your chosen security is going to move up to a new support point, known as point D, if not even higher.

- To work with this strategy, you want to have the stop loss end up at point C. If there is any time of the day where the price goes lower than your set point C, then you need to sell your stock and accept any losses that occur. The closer you can purchase the stock to that point C, the better with this strategy so that you can make sure your losses aren't too high.

- If you see that this stock continues to go higher, you will want to sell about half the position when it gets to point D. You can then move your stop higher to your entry point to help you make a profit.

- As soon as you see that the target is hit, or you see that the price is losing steam, even if it doesn't reach the goal, then you should sell the remaining shares that you have. When the price gets to a new low, this shows that the buyers are exhausted, and the trend will go backward.

There are a few steps that we need to follow to make this one work for our needs, but it is still a relatively simple process that even you as a beginner will be able to use and follow. However, to make it work as effectively as you would like, and to make sure that you can earn some profits from it, then you must have some patience. It is important with this one to only enter the markets at the right times, and to not get overly excited here, or you will end up losing a lot of money in the process.

Of course, we have to use some other caution here and be careful while watching the stock while you are in the trade, or you could miss out on a few things and lose a lot of money. It is possible that this trend can turn on you and start to go in a different direction than what you were planning, which is going to make it more difficult to work with and can cut into some of the profits that you want to make. But as a beginner who is looking to find a method to use that is simple and easy, then this is a good one to get started with.

The Shoulders and Head Patterns

Now it is time for us to move on to our third option to see how we are able to really make sure that we get some good results with our trading, and this is the head and shoulders pattern. This is a type of formation that you can notice on your graphs and charts that kind of looks like a baseline with three individual peaks. The two that fall on the outside should be similar in height, and then the one that falls right in the middle of them needs to be the highest.

This is a strategy that we are able to use in order to figure out if there is a trend reversal about to happen in the market or not. You can use it to see whether the trend reversal is bullish or bearish in nature as well. the pattern that you work with is going to include and be formed in three main parts, and all of them need t to be there to make sure that this trend works. The three parts that we need to spend some of our time on here to be prepared to use this strategy includes:

1. After the stock has gone through a bullish trend, you will see that the prices will reach a peak, and then there will be a decline. The decline that occurs is going to form a trough.

2. Then the price will rise again a little bit in order to form a second high, one that is actually quite a bit above the first peak, but then it will decline down again.

3. The price will come back up a third time. but it won't go higher; it will simply go to the same height, or similar, as the first peak before it declines down once more.

The first and the third peak are going to be the shoulders, and the second peak is going to form the head. And then there is a line that will connect together the first and second troughs, and this is known as the neckline.

You will find that it is possible to work with this kind of trend in order to see whether there is a downward trend that is about to happen, and that can help you to know when the prices are about to go back down. If you are worried about the prices going down because you own some of the stocks, this is a great way to get out of the market and maintain your profits. But if you are trying to get into the market, you would want to look for one of these to tell whether it was a good time to enter the market or not.

Working with the Moving Average

The next option that we will take a look at is the moving average trend. This is a good one that helps us to know whether a security is about to go up or down, and can help us to see the best time to enter into a trade and the best time to get out. This is important because it is a good way to be prepared and come up with the plan that you want to use on a variety of different securities.

Remember that there are many stocks out there that you can choose from, and many of them will have their own morning trend that you can watch for, either going up or down really strong. You would then want to watch their charts and see where the moving averages head on the charts. This can be a beneficial thing to work with because the trader simply needs to watch these moving averages to learn more about how the trend is occurring. Then they can jump in at the right times and ride it out until they make profits.

Chapter 9: Stocks and Option Trading

There is a big difference between options trading and stock trading.

Stock represents partial ownership of the company implying that when you purchase a stock, you are normally a part of the company. On the other hand, options trading is merely any ownership of a certain company; it is a contract involving a trader and another party that allows the trader to purchase or sell a certain amount of stock at a particular price within a specific period. The market may be so volatile but the strike prices reads are so high, and when the market activities are depicted to be calm, the strike prices may eventually be so down.

Let us look at some of the major differences between options trading and stock trading:

- Options tend to expire as depicted by the availability of expiration dates, while, on the other hand, stocks are much durable since they are properties of the company and bear no expiration dates. Therefore, stock trading is likely to happen for a longer period as compared to stock trading.
- Options derive the actual value from the value of the other assets involved during options trading, whereas stocks have a definite actual value that is fully recognized by the company in question.
- In the options trading activities, traders just have the full rights of the value amount. On the other hand, stock trading gives the traders gain full ownership of the property involved during trading activities.
- In options trading, the market predictability does not necessarily depend on the rates of supply and demand levels as compared to stock trading. With this in mind, the options trader is unlikely to predict what is happens to the market but he/she can, however, check on the volatility of the market.
- Options are much cheaper than stock. Money is so fundamental in trading and is always the biggest motivation in any kind of trading activity. Options are less expensive since the trader gets to acquire 100 shares of the equity during trading. Moreover, the cost of grasping an option contract is much cheaper as compared to purchasing and the underlying stock, and the trader acquires more amounts of benefits as compared to stock trading.
- Options are normally a great leverage tool in maximizing the amounts of profits gained during a particular trading period as compared to stock trading. This is evident in the collection of various amounts of premiums during the issuance of contracts hence increasing the amounts of profits collected in options trading as compared to stock trading.
- Options trading is much good at flexibility as compared to stock trading as evident in its tactical operations that happen frequently in various trading activities. Traders can make smaller investments that lead to good amounts of profits and fewer risks involved during a particular period. On the other hand, stock trading calls for good investments with multiple amounts of risks over an unspecified period.
- Another point is that options have a great chance of limiting the risks that are likely to be involved during trading, as compared to stock trading, where risk is pretty much unlimited during the unspecified period of trading.
- Options trading can better for you if your timing is okay, and as an options trader, you will be able to acquire larger amounts of profits during the contract as compared to when you would be involved in options trading.

- Options trading allows a particular option trader to bet where the market will not go—an activity that is not allowed in stock trading. The advantage of this opportunity is that there are higher chances of success than betting on where the market will go.

Terminologies:

Call option - This is an equity agreement that awards a buyer the chance to purchase 100 particular shares at a particular strike price within a specified time. A seller is also needed to sell off the stock at a particular price if the option gets exercised.

Commission - This is the fee charged in an options trading market after option orders have been executed on a securities exchange.

Option - It is a contract that allows an investor to purchase and sell a specific trading stock at a particular price within a particular period.

Strike price - This is the actual amount of price in which you choose to sell or buy options when you decide to exercise an option in the market.

Expiry date - This is the actual date–day, month, or year–to which a particular options trading contract becomes invalid and null.

Equity option - It is a kind of option that gives the owner, who happens to be the buyer, the chance to purchase and sell any available stock in the trading market at a specific share during a particular period before the expiration date is reached.

Time decay - This is the erosion period when the value of time of a specific option diminishes as the expiration date reaches.

Put option - The kind of option where a buyer is given the privilege to sell 100 shares at a constant price before the expiration date. On another hand, the seller of a put option is required to purchase stock at a particular price if the trading option gets exercised at all.

Volume -This is the number of contracts that have been traded during a particular options trading period.

Holder - The specific owner of the contract is referred to as the holder in options trading.

Long Option - This simply implies having purchased an option at online transactions and therefore own it.

Short Option - This means to have sold the option in an opening transaction.

Change - The percentage term price of the last hour's sale in the options market.

Index option - This is an option contract where the index is the underlying stock and not shares of any specific stock.

Time value - It describes the value to which time is attributable in options before a particular expiration date is reached.

Volatility - This is the actual fluctuation of prices of stocks in options trading where the stock prices keep rising and falling within time hence making it hard for traders to predict on future likely activities.

Contract - This is an agreement set between a buyer trader and a seller trader during a particular options trading activity.

Ask price - This is the lowest price that is being advertised in the options trading that anyone is willing to accept when selling a particular option at a particular period.

Last sale - It is the latest price that a certain option trader has traded within options trading.

Open interest - This is the number of the option that has been sold and also the ones that have not been brought back or in any case, exercise.

Bullish - This term is particularly referring to an investor who believes that a specific stock price will go higher or simply the market will rise higher.

Bearish - This term, on the other hand, describes a trader who believes that the market prices will do lower or the market will experience a downfall at a particular trading activity in a specific period.

Break-even point - This is the specific price that an underlying asset must reach to avoid the option buyer from acquiring losses if at all they decided to exercise the option.

Downside risk - This is the estimation of a particular downfall market price that is likely to be experienced by the market during the end of a particular trading period.

Implied volatility - This is an estimation of the future likelihood market volatility by analyzing the market status through the current activities occurring at the options trading market. Some traders get to use this as one of their strategies the options trading market to acquire large chunks of profits.

Index option - This is a kind of an option contract whose underlying security is an index and not shares of any specific stock.

Writing an option - This is to sell a call or put option contract that has been not possessed by any other trader in the market.

Mean - This is a mathematical operation where the total sum of observations in the market is divided by the particular number of observations in the market. The mean is used to provide data on various market values and the market standard deviation.

Spread - This is an option position established when a purchase of one option is established and a sale of an option too using the same underlying asset available in the trading market.

Historical volatility -This is analyzing the actual volatility of the past market occurrences and making the necessary helpful strategies and learning in your trading plan.

Credit - It is any value amount received in a particular trading account from the financial benefits experienced in various options trading activities. The profits and multiple benefits feed the trading accounts.

Debit - This is any amount of cash paid out to purchase an option during a particular trading period.

Horizontal - This is a term describing the options of the same strike price experienced in different months.

At the money - This term is used to describe the nearest price to the equity price during a particular trading moment.

Resistance - This is a particular level where the equity price cannot beyond any way higher, meaning that that particular price is the actual price limit.

Big chicken trade - This is a term used to describe a series of bull call calendars and the bear put calendars.

Ex-dividend - This is the actual date in which the stock enters the options trading market with the absence of dividends.

Selling to open - This ideally describes the selling of a particular option to open a position.

Selling to close - Selling a close means selling a specific option with the desire to close a particular position during options trading.

Bid spread- This is the actual difference between the asking price and the bid price for a given option during a particular options trading period.

Dip in the money - This is a term used to refer to multiple in-the-money occurrences that have been experienced in a particular trading period in the options market.

Option spread - It is established by buying and selling equal amounts of options of a similar class with the same underlying security. However, the strike prices and expiration dates of the options are different.

Stock - It is described as a portion of a particular company belonging or ownership.

Margin - This is a particular amount of loan offered by a particular broker of a specific trader during a particular trading period.

Trading platform - This is a general trading site that traders interact with while making trading moves, buying, selling, and any other trading activities. Trading platforms consist of various kinds according to different variety of interests, and a trader gets to pick on a site in which he or she is most comfortable with.

Chapter 10: How Does Day Trading Actually Work

In this chapter, we'll take a deeper look at how day trading really works. We'll start by comparing it to another popular form of trading: swing trading.

The primary difference between swing trading and day trading is the time frame for holding on to positions. Swing trading involves holding on to a position in financial securities for a minimum of one day, i.e., overnight, to several weeks. And in some cases, swing trading positions can take a couple of months to close because the expected price swings are much greater. As a consequence, the expected returns per trade are much higher.

Another difference between the two are the kinds of securities traded. Day trading focuses on securities with volatile price movements within the day while swing trading focuses on securities whose prices are expected to go up significantly over a much longer period of time than a couple of minutes or hours.

Hence, you shouldn't trade the same securities if you plan to do swing and day trading simultaneously. It's like saying you'll use a pair of running shoes for both running a 10-kilometer fun run and playing basketball. You can't use the same pair of shoes here.

Always keep the primary rule of day trading in mind: never hold on to a position overnight, even if it means taking a loss on trades.

But why do you have to stick to this rule even if it means suffering trading losses? After all, isn't making money the point of day trading?

Yes, making money is the point of day trading. But given that the ideal securities to day trade are volatile ones, holding on to them overnight can put you at high risk for greater losses the next day. It's ok to take small losses on day trades than large ones when you try to hold on to day trading securities overnight in the hopes that prices will recover greatly the next day.

By closing your position at the end of the day, even at a loss, you get to minimize day trading losses. And if you close positions at a profit, awesome! Don't feel like you could earn more by waiting until tomorrow. Remember, a bird in the hand's better than three in the bush.

You'll also need to remember that trading is a lot different than regular investing. While trading is a form of investing, regular investing usually refers to a more passive, buying- and- holding strategy that waits for months and years before taking profits. Trading has a much shorter time frame, which is only several hours for day trading and a couple of months at most for swing trading.

The Long and Short of Trading

When you buy a financial security, you take a long position on that security. When you hear a trader say that he or she's long 100 shares Intel stocks, it means that trader bought and is currently holding a hundred shares of Intel's stocks.

The point of taking a long position on a financial security is selling them later on at higher prices. To close a long position, you sell the securities you're holding.

When you sell securities that you don't own yet, you take a short position on that security. When you hear a trader say he or she shorted or sold short 100 shares of Intel stocks, it means that trader sold 100 shares of Intel stocks, hoping that its price will continue dropping so he or she can buy it back at a much lower price. It's the same principle as buying low and selling high, except that the "selling high" part comes before the "buying low" part.

How can you sell something you don't have and more importantly, why would you even do that?

First, let's answer why you should do that? And the answer is: to make money when prices of securities are dropping. As mentioned earlier, it's just a reversal of the general trading strategy of buying securities at low prices and selling them at higher ones. By selling securities while their prices are high and buying them later on at lower prices, you can trade profitably even during market downturns.

Now, how can you do it? Depending on your broker and whether you're qualified, you can borrow the securities from your broker, sell them, buy them back when prices drop, and return the securities you borrowed from your broker. In the process, you profit from the short sell.

To give you a clearer example of this, let's say the price of the cryptocurrency Bitcoin is falling but you don't have any Bitcoins with you at the moment. If your cryptocurrency exchange/broker allows it, borrow 1 unit of bitcoin and sell it for, say, $7,000. When the price drops further to, let's say,

$6,000 during the day, buy that one unit back and pay back your broker/exchange. In the process, you get to earn $1,000 in just one trade!

Keep in mind, however, that just like taking long positions, short selling also has its risks, which include that prices may actually go up instead of continuing to go down. In that case, you may also suffer trading losses.

You may be wondering, why would brokers or exchanges lend securities to their clients for short selling instead of selling the securities themselves? That's a very good question. And the answer is: brokers usually want to take long term positions on securities. Why?

Why take risks with short-term trades on a downward trending market when they can make money with much lower risks by simply lending it to customers who want to short sell for a fee. This way, everybody wins. The long-term investors get to keep their securities and profit, even during bear markets, while those who don't own securities can have opportunities to make profitable trades via short-selling.

Securities in Play

There's a reason why many investors, traders and analysts focus on market movements or indices. It's because they know that for the most part, most financial securities follow the overall trend of their respective markets unless they have a very good reason not to. For example, the prices of most stocks in the NYSE tend to go up when the Dow Jones is trending upwards and vice versa.

However, there will always be outliers that will – for one reason or another – go against the general trend for some specific reason. When their general markets are tanking, they're picking up. When their general markets are picking up, their tanking.

These securities are called securities in play (SIP). As a retail or individual day trader, these are the securities you should focus on within your chosen day trading market.

If you want to day trade stocks, these are stocks that buck the general trend of the NYSE or the Nasdaq. If futures contract, these will be futures contracts that go against the general trend of most other similar contracts.

You get the drift, right? Right!

What are some of the reasons that may account for the contrarian behavior of SIPs? These may include:

Unexpected results of earnings;

Surprise company or economic developments; and Major policy changes by the governing authorities.

So, just because a particular security bucks its general market trend doesn't mean you can consider it a SIP. There should be an underlying reason for the contrarian movement. If none, it's probably not a SIP.

Always remember another important day trading rule, particularly for choosing SIPs to day trade: Find out if a particular security's movement is due to general market sentiment or is it due to some unique fundamental reason?

For this, you'll need to do your homework. As a beginner day trader, you may have to do a bit more research than what you're accustomed to. But as you become a more experienced day trader, you'll be able to easily distinguish when a particular security is just going with the general market flow or when it's trending based on a unique and specific reason.

Professional day traders are those who do this type of trading for a living. While other forms of trading can sometimes be done as a hobby or a gambling high, day trading is often not included here. This makes them equipped to recognize changes in the market and to learn the trends of various industries, helping them to pick out the right trades to make money with day trading. Experience and some knowledge about the marketplace. If you don't have a good understanding of the market and its fundamentals, you will most likely lose money.

Enough money to start.

You need to have some savings or other money that you can put towards day trading. Make sure this is money that you can afford to lose. This helps to keep some emotions out of the trade and can help you make smarter choices with your trades. Often, you will need a large amount of capital is needed to capitalize effectively in this type of trading.

A good strategy

A trader needs to have a way to beat out the rest of the market. There are many strategies (some of which we will talk about later) that can help you with day trading. Each of them can be effective; you just need to pick the one you feel comfortable with.

Discipline.

All day traders need to have some discipline. If you aren't able to stick with your chosen strategy, then you will lose money. Success is virtually impossible without some discipline.

Chapter 11: Selecting a Broker

Who Is A Broker?

This is someone who buys and sells goods or things on behalf of someone else. They mostly are middle men in transactions, that often they make profit out of. They only have to organize and plan for transactions to take place between a purchaser/buyer and a vendor/seller. The broker ends up getting a commission out of the deal, either from the buyer or seller. Most of the time they represent the seller.

Brokers may be individuals or firms. When it is a firm, it still acts as a go between their customer and the vendor.

Brokers exist in many different industries. An example would be real estate brokers who advertise and sell properties on behalf of the owners. We also have insurance brokers who sell insurance on behalf of firms. We have stock market brokers who work on the stock market.

Why Use A Broker?

There are a few advantages of using brokers in any kind of business. As usual, before getting into any business with a broker, always do intensive research on what you are about to get into. There are a few bad crops in the market.

1. They know their market well

Most brokers are people or firms who have been in the field for quite a while and always know what is best for one client to the other. They also know who to talk to if you need anything specific and always do it well knowing they will benefit.

Brokers have been on the market for a long time and have seen what goes on and know too well what to expect. They have all the information you need right from the time you enter the market to the time you leave. They are particularly important when you are entering a foreign market that you aren't familiar with. You need to take time and look for the perfect broker that will tell you what you need and how to do things the right way. However, you need to be wary of the brokers who are out to exploit you. Use referrals and other methods to try and get the right broker who understands your needs.

2. Wider representation

A client is able to reach more people or a wide marker when using a broker, compared to them doing it by themselves. Brokers are also quite affordable, and have a network they work with; hence there is limited cost incurrence with them. Because most of them are well known, they are able to reach a wider market ratio easily.

When you decide to work with a broker, you get to cast your net wider so that you can get better business. Coming up with a network takes time, which is why it is just right that you work with a person that already has a network which you can tap in. This saves you time and effort, as well as money. Take time to work with a broker that already has a network of established clients.

3. Special skills and knowledge

Brokers mostly have special knowledge of the field they are in and are good at the specific brokerage area. This is because they work in detail so as to know the needs of different types of clients. Because of this, they are an asset to anyone who is looking for their services.

The skills that a broker has vary from customer relationship management to money management. They will help you to grow your empire as you sit and wait for them to do the work you want. It takes experience and a lot of patience for you to learn the skills and be able to do the things that a broker can do. So, always make use of a broker when making trading decisions.

4. Customer choice

Brokers always work with the customer's choice. They will always want to know what one needs they will always endeavor to ensure the customer is satisfied and has what they originally wanted, or better.

5. Time saving

Because they mostly know their trade well, a broker would be able to achieve more within a shorter period of time for the customer. This is because of their great networking within their field of specialization. They always know where to find what, at what time and for what amount.

The time that you save when you work with a broker can be used to handle other tasks that you have. Take time to make sure the broker knows what they are doing otherwise you will end up wasting a lot of time.

Types of Brokers
- Stock broker
- Business broker
- Pawn Broker
- Information broker
- Insurance broker
- Investment broker

Roles Played by Brokers in Forex Trading

For a long while, people have been quite skeptical about the Forex market, but this is something that has been growing rapidly the last few years. Forex trading has become one of the leading markets in the trading world. It generally involves the process of changing one currency to another for certain reasons. Currencies trade against each other depending on the exchange rates and brokers use the growth on these rates to make profits.

Because of this, there has been a high need of Forex brokers who are the middle men for investors who want to invest in Forex. Forex brokers are usually people or firms that provide currency traders with a platform to buy and sell their currency. They end up controlling a small portion of the large Forex market.

Their importance varies from need basis:

1. Link between the trader and the market

There are many investors who have a lot of funds and want to grow their wealth in Forex trading, but have no idea how to go about it. This is where brokers come in, and act as their representatives in the Forex market. Brokers know all the nooks and crooks of Forex trading, and always know when to take advantage of the exchange rate changes. They are best placed to give advice on how to go about trading, as they are always doing it as a day job hence very experienced.

Brokers always know when to take advantage of the market and the different events that would lead to an increase or decrease in the exchange rate, and hence know when to make the right moves. This they do at a smaller fee, so their aim is to have as many clients as possible so they can thrive on numbers.

2. Help educate investors or other beginner brokers

Brokers have lots of information on trading than most people would, and it is advisable for any beginner to have one to share tips with them. They would know how to go about avoiding some basic mistakes people make when they start investing in Forex markets.

3. They trade and negotiate on behalf of investors

Brokers are mostly the same as sales representatives. They trade currencies online, and the skilled ones do it as a daily job hence very useful for any beginner investor.

There are very many investors who want to trade but have no time, hence use brokers who do it full time. The Forex market is a 24-hour business operation and the exchange rates tend to rise and drop every moment. This means anyone trading has to always be on standby to make a move. Brokers do this on behalf of other people who have the money to invest but have no time.

This as times is most ideal as the brokers always know the right moves that bring in profits and incase of losses, they always know the move to make to reduce the amount of losses made.

4. Advise traders on risks that come with Forex trading

Forex trading, just like any other trading in the stock market, is a risky affair. As it highly involves currency values, there are times that the fluctuations can affect the market and a broker should be keen enough to know the right move to make.

Every investment has pros and cons, which are risks that investors will encounter one way or the other. One might lose more than the value of their transaction, but with a skilled broker to guide you through, you might be able to salvage the situation.

Major risk factors one might encounter:

Exchange rate risk: this is the risk that comes by as a result of changes in the value of the currency. There is a constant shift on the worldwide supply and demand balance, which might end up affecting the traders' position. This mostly depends on whichever way the currencies will move based on different factors. It is in this case where a broker advises one to cut losses early enough by taking different positions. These could be the position limit or loss limit. Other risks include:

- Interest rate risk
- Credit risk
- Country risk
- Liquidity risk
- Transactional risk
- Risk of ruin

5. Customer support during local trading hours
6. Ideas on latest trading platforms

Before you can work with a broker, you need to choose one. Choosing a broker isn't an easy task at all because you have hundreds of brokers to choose from. The best thing to do in this case is to try and make sure you work with referrals and testimonials when making a decision. Based on facts when getting the right broker.

Chapter 12: Day Trading Tips for Beginners

If you already have a basic understanding of stock trading in general prior to picking up this book, you can see that broadly speaking, day trading and stock trading are fairly similar. You make sure you have the capital, you find the right broker that fits your needs, and you do the research to make sure that the stocks in which you're looking to trade are going to prosper ultimately. This chapter will focus on the areas of day trading that differ from the broader points of stock trading. The tips presented in this chapter will provide you with concrete ways to increase the likelihood that you'll be successful through the avenue of day trading. Later chapters will focus on specific strategies that you can use to target the day trading market as a whole, and you'll be able to add these nuanced tips to any broad strategy that you ultimately choose to take.

Day Trading Tip 1: Only Purchase Shares when You Have

One important lesson that all stock traders must take to heart is the idea that they are essentially gambling their money on the New York Stock Exchange or on another trading floor. The money that you spend here is potentially money that you're never going to get back, and you should be purchasing shares and engaging in trade deals with this in mind. Regular stock traders at least have the luxury of being able to hold onto a bad stock to see if it will appreciate over a longer period of time. This is not the case for day traders. Additionally, many smart investors have a retirement or savings fund that they're looking to grow. They keep this money separate from the money that they're playing on the market. Consider adopting this sort of mindset. If you do make the decision to trade money that is from a retirement or savings fund, make sure that the trade is a fairly conservative one. Often, day trading does not allow of much conservatism. Keep this in mind as you decide on how much money to spend.

Along these same lines, recognize that day traders are typically purchasing many different stocks throughout the day. This means that you should be spending less money per stock than you would if you were trading more infrequently. Thinking about your finances in this manner will force you to begin to think in the short term rather than in the long term. There's no reason to purchase an expensive day stock, unless you have a fair idea that it's going to increase in value by the end of the day. The last thing that you want, especially as a new day trader, is for your money to vanish before you even have the chance to get used to everything that encompasses day trading.

Day Trading Tip 2: Be Ready to Go!

One of the biggest problems that many beginnings day traders face is actually having the courage to get started. Often, a new day trader will spend so much time analyzing their potential stocks and comparing themselves to other traders in the industry that they get cold feet. If you feel yourself acting similarly to the characteristics that were described above, resist the urge to back out of day trading altogether completely. After they've actually started to trade, one of the other problems that some new day traders have is that they spend so much time watching their screens for the right opportunity to present itself that when it does, they don't act decisively enough. Between fifty to seventy-five percent of all-day trades take place in a matter of seconds. Stick to your strategy, and if the moment that you should be acting presents itself, make your move. If you end up miscalculating the trade, know that there's something that isn't working in your plan and go back to the drawing board. If you adhere to the first tip that's presented in this chapter and only spend money that you can afford to lose, making a beginner's error won't be that big of a deal anyway.

Day Trading Tip 3: Find your Discipline and Stick to It

Once you have figured out the type of trading plan that you want to be using, it's important that you don't stray from your intentions. Especially when you first begin to day trade, impulses might be able to get the best of you. Even if your instinct is telling that a particular trade is a good idea, you might be going against traditional day trading principles by engaging in the deal. This is why it's important to not only have mentor or a teacher prior to engaging in day trading, but it's also important to stick to the strategy that you have in place. This is where the emotional and abstract concepts of fear and greed can come into play.

For example, if you were to exit from a deal out of fear even though you know that your strategy is telling you to keep your money in the trade for a bit longer, you are going against your doctrine. If you end up going freestyle and working off of instinct alone, there's a chance that fear will lead you to miss out on a great money-making opportunity. Contrastingly, if your strategy is telling you that it's time to let one of your shares go because the market is taking a turn for the worse, greed might be the little devil that's keeps you from pulling the plug. The result to this type of decision could result in the loss of money that didn't have to be gone if you had simply stuck with what you had learned. Be disciplined and let your strategy be the ultimate deciding factor on which stocks stay and which stocks go.

Day Trading Tip 4: Patience is Always a Virtue

One factor that may turn out to be the most perplexing or surprising for you to find out is that day traders sometimes do not trade every single day. Sometimes, if a day trader is sitting as his or her computer but don't see any opportunities that fit within their strategy, they'll watch the market without doing much at all. Many day traders, when they're first starting out, feel as if they need to constantly be trading at the sake of their better judgement or overall plan that they've implemented. A great mantra that is often heard within the day trading world is one that goes like this: Plan Your Trade, Then Trade Your Plan. Be sure that the trades that you're making fit within the overall structure that you've created for you and your goals, and don't be hasty just because you aren't seeing anything that's worth your trouble.

Day Trading Tip 5: Enter into a Trade when the Supply and the Demand for a Stock are Drastically Imbalanced

If you've ever taken an introduction to economics class (it's likely that you have if you're interested in stock trading), one of the key elements to this type of class is the theory of supply and demand. This theory pertains to the stock market as much as it does the economy as a whole. When demand is high and it seems as if every single investor is looking to purchase a particular stock because it's the "hot" commodity during a given period of time, it's almost guaranteed that the price of this stock is going to rise because of the increase in demand in conjunction with a limited supply of shares. Contrastingly, when demand is low and the market is saturated with shares that seemingly nobody wants, the price of that stock is going to be relatively low. Having this basic sense of what's going on regarding supply and demand within the stock market will provide you with a better ability to track when a particular share is going to increase or decrease in price. All you have to do is track the historical price of the stock over the relatively short period of time and make sure that you're researching the climate of the company when you're looking to buy. For example, if PlayStation 2 was about to unleash a new gaming system on the world, it might be a good idea to purchase a share of this stock as investors prepare for this release. You have a feeling that demand for a PlayStation product is going to be high, so you can also assume that the shares of a PlayStation stock are also going to grow. If you can pinpoint a point in time when the shares of a certain company are going to become more or less saturated with other investors, this will help you to plan accordingly.

Day Trading Tip 6: Set Price Limits Before You Start Trading

Think about it. If you don't set target prices for yourself, how are you going to be able to determine when you should be trading a particular stock? While it sometimes can be okay for a regular stock trader to purchase a particular stock without having a clear notion of exactly how much money he or she is willing to lose potentially, it's at least possible for these types of investors to figure it out over a long period of time. Day traders do not have this luxury.

Before you even get to the point of trading, you should be deciding how much of a profit would be acceptable to you, as well as exactly how much money you're willing to lose on one particular trade. Of course, everyone wants to make as much money as possible through the stock market, but the reality is that there are limits to how much you can make through each transaction, especially when you're partaking in day trading. Instead of going into a trade with the mindset of "I'm going to make tons of money through this deal!" try to push yourself to think about your stocks a bit more rationally. Look at the stock's history and figure out on average how much it has been making for other investors in the past. Then make your decision, and stick to it. It's perhaps even more important to determine how much you're willing to lose on a particular trade before calling it quits. If you set a stopping point for yourself, it's less likely that you'll find yourself in a situation where the stock has plummeting and you're still holding onto the debt remains of its corpse.

Day Trading Tip 7: Understand and Use the Risk-Reward Ratio

Our final day trading tip involves a concept known as the risk-reward ratio. The risk reward ratio, in its most basic sense, means that the ratio that you win from a particular trade should outweigh the risks that are associated with the trade by a certain amount. For day trading in particular, you should be looking to calculate a risk-reward ratio that is 1:3, meaning that the reward associated with the risk is three times greater than any risk that could become a problem. Of course, this ratio is not determined simply through arbitrary means. Instead, the risk-reward can be mathematically determined. When you're looking to figure out the risk-reward ratio, you need to numbers.

Chapter 13: Psychology and Mindset

Day Trading, like any other form of investment, is subject to influence from human emotion and psychological impact. Whenever money or capital is in play, people tend to take matters rather personally because of the inevitable consequence of the hope that comes along with the promise of significant returns. People will strive to make money while at the same time, avoid circumstances that may cause them to lose their capital. It is from this zero-sum mentality that the influence of psychology or emotions may creep into a sensible mindset. Such control takes over every aspect of the Day Trading instincts that you learned over time.

Your knowledge goes out of the window when a situation that triggers your psychological response arises. A high degree of counterproductivity thus ensues. It, eventually, leads to the dismissal of logical decisions in favor of hunches as well as the need to chase after fleeting profits and cover your previous losses. For you to manage your Day Trading expertise through challenging scenarios, you need to look out for emotions that alter your reasoning capability adversely. Try to improve and nurture a productive mindset, while at the same time, avoid promoting a mental culture that justifies negativity falsely. The following few behaviors and traits are central to your particular mindset whenever you decide to participate in Day Trading:

Do Not Rationalize Your Trading Errors

This mindset t is one of the leading obstacles to the progress and eventual success of your Day Trading endeavors. You are often prone to justify any trading mistakes that you make to the detriment of moving forward. For instance, you get an entry into a particularly promising trade deal later than necessary in spite of your much earlier knowledge of its potential for profitability. The delay causes you to miss an excellent opportunity at the previous entry point. However, you decide to justify this misstep by convincing yourself of your preference for trading late over missing the same deal entirely.

The downside to such delays is often a faulty sense of size estimation in taking your trading position. Hence, the resulting increased exposure to financial risk you become disadvantaged by. Beware of your procrastination when it comes to productive openings that are currently available in Day Trading. If you possess this tendency, consider getting rid of it as soon as possible before it costs you a lot more capital in the long run. In case you are not prone to the frequent postponement of your responsibilities to a later date, be alert for the development of this mentality with the trading company that you keep. You can quickly become influenced by the kind of traders from whom you seek advice on more complex trading strategies. When present, stockbrokers affect your trading ethos, as well.

Poor trading etiquette from these external sources will rub off on you and vice versa. Try to keep the company of well-known responsible trading partners and stockbrokers when the need arises. Another rationalization scenario involves a run of profitable results. Based on a series of trade deals that made you successive returns, you begin to convince your brain of your seemingly high intelligence. This false belief in your skills may lead you to overestimate your trading expertise. Before long, you may start engaging in Day Trading on a hunch rather than apply logic to your decisions. You stop referring to your trusted trading plan and jump into many trading opportunities haphazardly. After a while, these instances of carelessness and trading arrogance will catch up with you because they always inevitably do. Your chances of plunging into a financial disaster go up.

With your eventual financial ruin come the cases of psychological meltdown leading to a negative feedback loop. A wrong decision from your misplaced sense of conceitedness will invariably lead to high-risk exposure. As a result, you suffer significant losses eventually, and consequently, your emotional health suffers, causing you to spiral into a state of depression. This loop is often self-propagating, meaning that it feeds onto itself. Bad decisions lead to adverse outcomes and a fragile mindset, which, in turn, is prone to make more bad decisions, and the loop goes on and on. Keep in mind that in Day Trading, such a feedback loop is often disastrous. All these adverse effects arise from your initial false sense of justification for a wrong deed.

Beware of Your Trading Decisions

This advice is so apparent that it sounds redundant when mentioned. However, decisions are typically the product of your reasoning and judgment at a particular moment. When it comes to decisions on Day Trading, psychological influence is often a determining factor in the process. Keeping your wits about you is very crucial, especially when everything seems to be out of control. You need to realize that every trade has its ups and downs and how you deal with the challenging times is often more consequential. Try to maintain a logical mindset when making Day Trading choices from a variety of bad options. When it seems that an imminent financial downturn is inevitable, the extent of your loss becomes essential. In this case, you will need to make a sensible decision on the degree of losing margins that you can tolerate adequately.

At this point, you are probably in a state of so many overwhelming emotions that your foggy mental faculties become clouded. An expected human response is to run away from danger, naturally, but in certain situations, fleeing may not be an option. A reflex in a trading scenario often leads to an impulsive decision. Such a choice is, in turn, typically not well thought or deliberative. You should confront your unfavorable circumstances head-on and attempt to fix the situation, however hopeless. This sense of perseverance is usually the essence of most trading excursions, especially when the times become financially rough. Going through the loss of some capital and other Day Trading challenges is often a painful experience that can lead to illogical decisions.

Always remember to uphold vigilance and adhere strictly to the guidelines in your trading plan when confronted with obstacles during your trades. The trading plan usually has instructions on how to handle these seemingly desperate situations. In addition, the prior preparation of any trading guide is generally free of emotional or psychological influence; hence, you can rely on it to maintain neutrality. Also, beware of making trading resolutions when going through a phase with a foul mood. Such conclusions are bound to lead you into a financial catastrophe, especially if you are not careful. Learn to put off the verdict to a time when you can resume logical thinking. When you make any rash decision, it can only result in your further exposure to even more risk.

Keep Your Emotions in Check

Learn to stick to a Day Trading system and method that you trust. Such a strategy may be one that has a history of always making significant returns. Once you master and fully grasp how to apply a specific approach to your trading deals, try to fine-tune it to your preference based on your ultimate objectives. Afterward, stick to this tried, practiced, and tested system in all your searches for valid trade deals. On some days, the stock market may be slow with a low volume of trade. The volatility in such a case is often negligible. However, due to an unchecked emotional influence, you develop a sense of greed or lust for profits.

The desire for benefits on a slow day is common. It leads to the urge to trade on anything to make a small profit. In this situation, you will move from Day Trading into gambling. Trading requires a logical mindset on your part with a lack of psychological attachment whatsoever. Gambling is a consequence of emotional and mental factors running amok in your Day Trading system. If a particular trading style worked on multiple times in the past, teach your brain to consider it. Your trusted trading system will indicate a lack of valid trade opportunities on a specific slow market day. In this case, curb your emotions, desires, and urges to chase a quick profit; however strong they seem.

You should never allow yourself to resort to gambling under any circumstances. Gambling is detrimental to healthy and responsible Day Trading behavior. The risk exposure exponentially rises when you grow accustomed to the desire for profits. If a given day of trading is unfavorable, you should not take part in invalid and unworthy deals. In addition, you should only trade on verifiable opportunities. At certain times, you may experience a series of successive returns in a relatively short period. Learn to know when to stop and how to curb your lust for wanting more returns. Trust your system to trade only on valid deals; however, multiple opportunities are available. An emotion that goes unmonitored in such situations is the greed for more profit.

You convince yourself psychologically that the various deals could be a sign of your lucky day. This mentality in a false belief is wrong, and you need to be aware of it. Your psychology can play deceitful tricks on your logical mind leading to high-risk trading deals. You must realize that in Day Trading, it is almost impossible to get more returns out of a system than what the stock market offers. Emotional corruption also comes into play in a scenario where you bite off more than you can chew.

The greed for substantial amounts of returns may cause you to take high-risk trading positions for a chance at quick profits. However, you must remember that profits and losses are both possible outcomes from a Day Trading session. Therefore, you need to learn to trade in amounts that you can afford to lose. After all, Day Trading involves taking a chance based on a speculative position. You should practice trading in small amounts of money within the confines of low-risk deals. In this case, a potential loss may not be as damaging as the earlier high-risk trading position driven by greed. Eliminate the role of emotions in Day Trading and learn to accept the uncertainty of an unknown future outcome.

Be Patient When Trading

Patience is a crucial trait to have when you take part in Day Trading due to the upswings and downward trends in stock prices. It can become challenging to identify the right entry or exit point for a particular trading opportunity, given the fluctuating nature of a volatile market. However, when you master the art of being patient and studying the trade intently, you can come up with a winning strategy. Having a planned approach is essential, and you should prepare one before engaging in any Day Trading. Often, most seasoned traders include trading strategies for different market conditions in their trading plans. Hence, when making your trading plan, consider incorporating a trading strategy within it.

If unsure of how to proceed, you can always seek the assistance of qualified stockbrokers. They have the experience of encountering various Day Trading scenarios in the real world. If trustworthy, they could provide you with invaluable insights on coming up with a proper strategy. Now it is up to you to stick to the plan in every session in which you participate.

Chapter 14: What Should You Invest in to Be Profitable at Day Trading

Day trading is never the same for each day. A trader that has been trading for a length of time that is longer than a year will find that there is never two single days that are the same. Even though there are no similarities to the day, there are still patterns to the trends. They will occur over time, but they will be hidden within a random movement of price that takes place daily.

There are five-day setups that can occur over a specific amount of days, and at least one to two will occur within one day's time frame. However, they will not all occur in the same days' time period. Learning these trade setups will help you to exploit the potential of profit.

Context within the Patterns

Know the pattern and watching are not going to be enough for a successful day trading. These patterns will occur frequently; however, they only hold power when a specific context appears. Understand the action price in order to have a great entry in day trading. Identify when the traders are stuck, and the price will have cause to surge in a direction that is forced, meaning that the traders are selling. These setups will occur during emotional points. This is when traders will feel the pain or the greed. However, there is not going to be a definite that this will occur prior to big moves and it does not mean that there will be a result of big moves. We do not have an exact knowledge of what the traders think, or if the acts will take place based on these thoughts. By watching the action of the price patterns, you will see regular occurrences. These can produce results that are similar, which can improve the chance that the trade is profitable.

Impulse Buys Create Pullback That Results in a Consolidated Breakout

Trading can begin in a move that is strongly pulled in one single direction. This will take place within 5-15 minutes once the market opens for trading. The Stock Market calls this impulse wave. The price of the stock then will pull back and then stall out. This forms the consolidation so that the price will move sideways for about 3 minutes. It must occur within an impulse wave range. The pullback or consolidation has to occur lower than the price of open. Due to the initial impulse's direction, the investor will wait and experience the breakout that leaves the consolidation in the direction that is equal to the stock. Breakouts that head in the opposite direction are not traded. You want to consolidate and pull back if the price is rallied as soon as it opens. Next, you should wait for that price to be above the consolidated breakout price, and then the long trade is triggered. Consolidation must be, compared to others, small in relation to the impulse wave that is going to precede it. The pattern becomes less effective when the consolidation is compared to the large impulse wave. During the pullback, there should be a distinct pullback, as well as impulse waves that are distinct. If they are not distinct, then the effectiveness of the pattern is less and is avoided.

This pattern can be seen throughout the trading day and can be how a trend will form. This makes it a strategy that can be utilized on most frames of time and in the market. The most power-filled moves that a market will have will take place during the open of the day, which is why catching that first hour is important. It can mean important things for your portfolio and creates large impacts with your profitability. If it occurred later in the day, then it can create smaller moves in price.

Consolidation Reversal Breakout

Impulses are not always followed by pullbacks that are small. There can be big moves that head in one direction. However, they can grow in the movement to an even bigger direction that is opposite of the original one. This is a reversal in directionality. Focus on the big moves that are most recent.

If the price dropped to $0.20 at the open, then rallies at $0.30, do not get distracted with that first drop since it will not matter anyhow. You will now have what is called an impulse for the upside. Watch for the decline in price, just a bit, and then consolidate the stock. If the consolidation breaks $0.01 then stay longer. On the reverse, you can wait for the pullback to go to the opposite for the impulse. Then you will see the impulse has a smaller pullback.

Support/Resistance Reversal

This can be horizontal lines as well as diagonal lines. They will point you in a direction that the price has been reversed for at least 2 episodes prior. This will include that starting point. You should know that the support, as well as the resistance, is not a price exactly but an area. The setup is not required to take place near the support, nor the resistance. In other words, it can take place slightly below them or above them. This informs us to be on high alert, which is based on the fact that a reversal can be coming. Because of this, we will have to sit and wait for the consolidation that is near. There is a signal for trade if the break in price is above the support that is consolidation, or below consolidation that is resistant. If this signal occurs, the price of the trade that moved one cent higher than the consolidation close to the support and fall for resistance which occurs in the pattern. Leave the trade immediately if the resistance breaks above or below the support area. Consider that the trade of breakout could be applicable.

Breakout Area Is Strong

This is a fashionable way to trade a breakout that is either above or below the support major area. This is, however, one of the toughest. Although the strategies above are preferred, it is beneficial to explore strategic options for special situations that can arise. Look out for a level that has pushed back the price for multiple strategies that are basic. This price will rally and then will reach 25.25 however, and then it falls. Although it performs this dance several times, it can struggle to break through. Once the area has tested that price three times more, there can be an assured day trades that are noticed. Suddenly the price is reaching 25.26. This can signal shifts of importance. Breakouts do not guarantee moves that are big. You may fail to produce a move that is big, and the price can break boundaries that are strategic and sparing. By making moves away from the area, you should see a significant move away from the visual that is price tested. The pattern can lose the effectiveness that will significantly become rejected by the price that is near the area. This means that you should see several rejections that have happened over multiple times.

Once the traders push the level of the price back, it becomes a pattern of the power, despite the level that is sent. The price of the fact is opposite in direction for multiple occasions in the past. This shows that they have a greater resolve than the opposite directions the traders are going.

How Do You Make Day Trading Your Job?

If you have opened a broker account and begin to trade stocks, you are not required to have a license. If you plan to work for a firm to trade stocks, then you will need to acquire a series 7 license. This requires a specific number of hours in a classroom and then a test that will license you as a stockbroker. In order to sell and buy stocks for others, even as your own business, you will need the license. For your own personal financial gains, you can use an online brokerage account and earn money for yourself.

Series 7 Licensing is a test that is taken after you have completed a specific number of hours for training and learning. A job that involves trading stocks, bonds, and other securities and then you will need to follow the guidelines that are set up by the SEC. These regulations require you to have Financial Industry Regulatory Authority. This requirement states that you will need stock brokers and securities licensing representative. There are several options of FINRA registrations; however, the one that is most necessary will be the General Securities Registered Representative. This will require you to complete a class and pass the test that is called a series 7 exam. There are some limited exams that can provide you with limited securities capabilities. These allow you to trade specific bonds or options. Once you pass the proper test, you will complete the license requirements. This means that you can apply for your series 7 licenses.

In order to take the test and get licensed, you will need to have an employer sponsor you for the test. This means being sponsored by a FINRA member for the financial company service. You will need to be hired by a brokerage firm and then put through rigorous training and put you to work with a trading mentor. They will then sponsor you for the license as a securities trader. There are not that many pre-requisites that are required to be hired as a broker however, the licensing is required once you start to trade. Once you are hired you will have an agreement that states that you are employed only until and if you pass the series 7 test. The firm will oftentimes provide you with the training that is needed or the courses that will give you the ability to pass the test.

A self-employed trader is able to trade with no licensing requirements for trading within your own account with the broker. You have to use your own money and if you cannot make it a successful career then you will lose your new career. If you begin with a smaller account and then use that to learn as you go, you will be able to trade prior to turning this into your full-time work profitably. Then you can trade the day job for a profession that is full-time and profitable.

Many of the day traders are trading stocks, although it is just as popular for a day trade to trade bonds, as well as currencies or even commodities. You generally need to look for securities that have these features:

- A trade volume that is large and highly liquid.
- Bonds that are volatile. You want changes that are frequent for the price because this allows the investor to make a quick profit.
- Stocks that are known by you. You need an understanding of what that particular stock's history in price is, and various events that designate how it will react to— economic shifts or earnings reports. This is a key deciding factor. Day traders will often only trade a selected few specific stock, developing their expertise in the companies that they are trading. This will help them to narrow their focus so that they are not thinking too broad.

Chapter 15: The Dos and Don'ts of Day Trading

Day trading is a business that you can set up fast. The very first step is to define if you are a full-time or part-time day trader. In this chapter, I will explain the basic tips for day traders. I will shed light on what kind of weapons you are going to need along the way. I assume that you have allocated the budget that you want to invest in your trading business. The first rule of a trading business is that you should not trade with the money that, if lost, is likely to dent your lifestyle. This money, in the world of trading, is known as 'scarred money.' When you are trading with scarred money, fear comes to haunt your decisions and you lose more often a winning bet. Don't let fear color your business decisions. If you do that, you will be making the worst possible trading choices and lose money in the end. If you get the chance to interview traders and brokers, you will realize this fact.

The Do's of Day Trading Business

Here is a rundown of the things that you must do when you enter day trading business.

- The basic thing is to be persistent in your approach. You should keep going even amid adversity. Just think of the last time you have learned something worthwhile or fun. Remember how you behaved when you started playing baseball or fishing. Did you become a master the very first time you did that? Did you behave awkwardly or were you smooth in handling the equipment? Did the bat drop from your hands? Can you recall a person who mastered it the first time? Even if there is anyone, he would be one out of thousands. No one masters anything from the first attempt. You need time to build and polish your skills. You usually are pretty bad at first but you learn to make it right over time because you have an urge buried down in your heart to make it better. If you are desperate to become a musician, you will become one someday. Same is the case with day trading. It can be frustrating at the start. Don't try to give up on a couple of failed trades. You may lose some part of your capital while you desperately attempt to bag profits from a trade. If you have failed, you must push past this pain and keep your gaze fixed at the horizon. You must keep in mind the final destination. Only then you can get over the desperation and the frustration.

- When you make up your mind about making a career out of day trading, you should create a tangible and practical plan that you must strictly follow. Every business demands a strategic plan that you must build and evolve along the way. A good plan should contain all aspects of your trading strategy. Without a solid plan, you are not trading but gambling. So, don't just gamble. Follow set rules. Your plan may contain the timing of your trade, the amount of initial investment, the companies you want to invest in, the timing you want to hold a stock, and the time you will have to invest in studying technical reports, charts, and volumes of a given stock.

- Do prepare a checklist. A checklist usually is as much important as a trading plan. You need to include your trading rules in the list. You should be satisfied with the checklist before you enter a trade. For example, you can decide how much leverage you need to take and what should be the risk-reward ratio. Going through the checklist each time you make a new trade cuts down your chance of making any kind of silly beginner-level mistakes. Once you have done trading for a couple of months, all the points of the checklist will be fed in your brain, and you will not need them anymore.

- The next thing you should do is to follow a strict routine. Day trading is not like a job or physical business that binds you for a set period. Trading is a lonely endeavor and some of you may struggle after finding themselves in a new situation in which they are not under the watch of any kind and they are not being instructed on what to do. It is you who have to make decisions and shape your future. Therefore, you must have a routine. It will be risky for your capital and your business if you take long breaks from work during active hours of trading. You may miss out on high-probability opportunities. If you have set up a daily routine by clearly defining your goals, you can remain on track and build a successful career as an independent trader.

- If at any point you feel that you don't have sufficient learning, you should take time to learn. There is always room for that no matter how much you think you have studied books and online material. You can lose all your money in a matter of hours. The best learning approach is to learn the jargon at first and understand the basic concepts. You must know what a particular word means. Just think of an engineer! Can you call a person an engineer if he or she doesn't know what a particular word in the book of engineering means? What will you do if he has not attended the college of engineering but call himself an engineer? Would you trust him? Would you like them to build a bridge in your hometown? Would you like them to work on the flyover in your city? You will do everything a bit to keep them away from these projects. You will not hand over your house construction project to an engineer who has just graduated. You will find someone with lots of experience and knowledge. Similarly, you should do that the same when you start trading. Consider yourself as a novice engineer who knows a little and who also has little experience to his credit. When you have traded for a while, you will be able to develop a knowledge base that you can use to gain more knowledge such as to learn better and faster. Apply these initial concepts to your trading practices and improve your knowledge.

The Don'ts of Day Trading

Just like the do's, there are some don'ts of day trading as well. Here is a rundown of the things that you don't have to do if you want to survive in this business.

- The very first don'ts of day trading is emotional instability. If you feel that you lose emotional control easily and if you get angry or overly happy each time you try to make money, you are not following the recipe to success. A forex trader or stock trader cannot be angry or extremely happy. The best traders across the world are the ones who can part their emotions from trading. As a human, emotions are our weaknesses. We make mistakes when we get emotional. Don't let emotions carry you away and have greater control over what you buy and sell. It happens often when you make a big profit from a sale, you get happy and make a purchase that is triggered by euphoria rather than logic. It can wipe out the gains from your previous trade.

- If a person pays heed to rumors around him, the best method to deal with him is to ignore him. You will not like to talk to someone who always lends his ear to rumors about politics or other national issues. The same is true in the world of trading as well. You cannot listen to rumors and act on them. Well, it gets tempting to do so sometimes. Some scenarios fan rumors. For example, you are most likely to believe and act on rumors if you have invested a big amount in a particular stock and have not yet earned anything since morning and are desperate to earn before the day ends. You may feel tempted to heed to rumors if you have recently bagged profit by acting on a rumor. Your brain might convince you to repeat the practice again. Remember that you don't need to listen to rumors no matter whatever the scenario is. You must do in-depth research before you act on a rumor. You might have a friend who claims to be a master of trading and who has made lots of money and who is always ready to offer his advice, but it is not wise to always act on what he says. Your financial situation is always different from the situation of your friend. His trading strategy might be different. His capital might be bigger or smaller than yours. You don't always know what his stop-loss is or what his target price at which he would sell is. If he listens to a rumor and you follow suit, both of you will land in serious trouble. Similarly, don't always pay heed to what your broker says to you.

- The second don't that you must remember is that you should not isolate yourself from others. It is very natural for you to do so because it is the need of this business. There are two reasons as to why isolation happens in the first place. Day traders have to work from home and keep the focus on the latest analysis coming from different sources. The concentration and amount of study involved in it demand that you work in isolation. But is it healthy for you and your business? Isolation will take a toll on your mental and physical health hence there is a need to create joint working opportunities. Try to focus on teaming up with a group of professional traders who will provide each other support throughout the busy day. In this way, you will be able to get a sense of how other traders are approaching their business and how they are solving the problems that arise over the day. You will have the opportunity to collaborate and communicate amidst work, which will allow you to pick a bunch of tips. You will also be able to share your own experience with others. The last sentence may sound counterintuitive to you but the fact of the world remains that the more you give away, the more you receive. Your brain might have started telling you that you never trade your secrets, but that's half true. The things that have worked for you may not work for others because it is not only knowledge that matters in success but the conviction, the commitment, the focus, and the courage you pour in it that does the magic. Take it in the sense that when you create a culture of sharing, you invite others to share their thoughts as well. In this way, all members of a group can learn and grow.

Chapter 16: Trends

Trends are supposed to be a trader's friend, or so we've been told repeatedly by every single trading book out there. I agree with this thought. However, the issue is that very few traders can actually identify what a trend really is and how friendly it is in the moment.

Ask a beginner trader what a trend is and they're likely to point their arms at a 45-degree angle, either up or down, and call that a trend. The truth is that this is just one type of trend. Trends have varying degrees of strength attached to them and the 45-degree trend is just one of the many form's trends take. It also happens to be the friendliest.

One of the most difficult aspect of trading trends is that they can run away from you before you can take advantage of them. Prices move very quickly when trending and this is why, contrary to popular perception, trends are not very friendly to beginner traders. You need to be quick and decisive when entering a trend and both of these attributes are in short supply when we speak of beginner or unsuccessful traders.

However, by learning to identify the nature of the trend currently prevailing in the market (its strength), you'll be in a much better position to understand how you can take advantage of it. All trends go through three phases: The beginning, middle and end.

The three phases of trends have certain characteristics to them which you need to look out for. One of the reasons why it is extremely important for you to be able to identify these characteristics is that you'll know how much longer the trend is likely to proceed. By doing this, you can let your profits run as much as possible and get out before the trend ends and prices move in the other direction.

The Beginning

Trends begin from within ranges and this makes the beginning portion of a trend a little difficult to identify. You can't see this in Figure 5, but portion A is actually the end of a larger range. Don't worry about what a range is at this point. Just keep in mind that you don't need to get in on the very first bar of a trend. In fact, the best time to enter a trend is not at the beginning but during the transition period between the beginning and the middle.

The beginning of a trend doesn't usually look like one and in real time, it is unlikely you'll be able to spot it. However, there are some tell-tale signs to watch out for. The first is that price will begin to show definite bias towards one particular side of the market. In Figure 5, notice how the huge bearish bars to the left are not challenged by bulls. Price keeps meandering downwards, even if it does so while moving sideways for the most part.

Another tell-tale sign of the beginning of a trend is the sluggish nature of price movement that occurs after rapid changes. Box A is a perfect example of this. A few sharp bearish bars are followed by a bunch of small bars that take price nowhere. It's almost as if price is in two minds: It isn't sure whether to move down or move sideways. This kind if hesitation is caused due to bearish (in this case) traders absorbing any remaining bullish pressure before getting ready to push price down.

Lastly, notice the big bearish bars at the start of A. These bars are decently sized and aren't met with much support. The price drop is relatively smooth. What I mean is that price doesn't jerk downwards as much as it flows down. Keep this feature in mind for later.

The Middle

The middle is where the fun really is. This is where you'll make the most money if you can correctly identify the phase the trend is in. At some point towards the end of the first phase (the beginning) of a trend, the with trend traders (bears in this case) decide enough is enough and apply pressure on the market.

This results in price tumbling downwards. You can see this happen quite clearly towards the end of A and in the first half of B as the bears are pretty much unchallenged. In the first quarter of B, we see a massive upswing but this is the same upswing as such, this is an anomaly. Notice that price moves down quite forcefully and that bullish presence is negligible.

The second half of B is another story altogether. Here, we see the brakes being put on the trend as price begins to move sideways. The general movement is still towards the downside but there's no doubt that the bulls are reasserting themselves. Every bearish push is met with a counter bullish push, even if it isn't as strong as the downward pressure.

Towards the second half of the middle, the counter trend traders (in this case the bulls,) begin to find their voice so to speak. They assert themselves to a greater degree as they find that the bears aren't as strong as they once were. All of this set's things up nicely for the final phase of the trend.

Before we move to the end, I'd like to point out certain characteristics of the middle of a trend. The first half of the middle is dominated by the with trend side. The transition period from the beginning to the middle is a crucial phase where you need to prepare to enter.

Even if you miss the transition phase, the middle of a trend will still give you ample opportunities to enter.

So, where and how should you enter? Well, recall what you learned about SR levels. Can you spot a few SR levels where you can enter short (that is sell before buying the instrument back at a lower price?) Can you spot any levels which are retested from the opposite side once broken? In addition to this, there are a few price patterns that are printed as well which you'll soon learn about.

At this point, don't worry about figuring out where to enter. Your job is to understand and explore the phases of a trend. If you can spot a trend that is still in the beginning or in the middle, you will know that any counter trend pressure is likely to be short lived and that the correct thing to do is to ride the trend for as long as possible, until it starts displaying characteristics that indicate it is coming to an end.

The End

The end of a trend is marked by two types of price behavior. In Figure 5 we do see instances of both although this will not always be the case. The first type of behavior is called exhaustion. Exhaustion is when the growing counter trend (in this case bullish) pressure starts alarming the with trend traders (bears.) This causes them to gear up and seek to smother the bulls completely.

There's just one problem: The bulls are much stronger now and are not going to go away. Hence, the bears put even more effort into their push and in the process produce a huge downward move. The flip side is that in doing so, they exhaust themselves and have nothing left.

you can see this manifest as a huge bearish bar. This looks impressive but notice how nothing follows after this. A series of smaller bars follow and the bulls are still there. Sure, they don't immediately push back but remember, we're still in a bearish trend. Trends don't end on a dime and flip back in the other direction. There is a transition period.

Contrast the exhaustive downward movement with the bearish push in the beginning of the trend. While in the beginning, the downward moves were smooth and didn't have much push back, here, bearish moves are jerky and if they aren't huge enough, are immediately wiped out.

The second type of price behavior you will see towards the end of a trend is increased sideways movement. Whereas the beginning sees a general decrease of such movement, the end witnesses an increase. Notice how after exhausting itself, price moves sideways in little bars. Also notice how the bears try to push prices further down but they aren't able to do so. They just have no strength left.

The end of a trend is the best place to get out of your short position (or long in case of a bullish trend.) Ideally, you'll want to wait for the exhaustion but it doesn't always manifest as I mentioned earlier. Watch out for a lack of with trend progress and increasing sideways movement. Whatever you do, don't try to squeeze the last few bits of juice from the end of a trend.

Many traders fall into this trap and only end up wasting their time and energy. It's far better to instead prepare for the new state the market is moving into: A range. Before getting into ranges though, I'd like to point out a few things:

1. Conventional wisdom identifies just the transition period between the beginning and the middle as being a 'trend.' As you can see, a trend is much larger than that and contains ample sideways movement.

2. Don't worry about the exact transition period between phases. All that matters is that you understand the major characteristics and learn to watch out for them.

3. There is a difference in the sideways movement in the second half of the middle and in the end. The middle sees negligible counter trend progress. It's more about slowing the trend down. The end sees negligible with trend progress. Here, the counter trend traders might not make progress but neither do the with trend traders. This is because they're being absorbed by the other side.

Chapter 17: Money Management

The truth is that a lot of traders, especially novices, started with a lot in their trading accounts and at the end of the day, they had little or nothing to boast about. Many of them lost their funds because of thoughtless actions or not following a well-crafted strategy. To manage your money well, there are some things that you have to do.

Choose the Right Lot Size Based on Your Capital

When you start at forex training or financial market trading, you will tend to learn about trading lots. What we mean by a lot is the tiniest trade size available that can be placed when you decide to trade currency pairs on the foreign exchange market.

Usually, brokers tend to talk about lots using increments of a thousand or a micro lot. You have to understand that the lot size determines directly, as well as shows that risk among that you are willing to take.

Using a risk management calculator or a top like that can help you know what the right lot size is, based on what your trading account assets are currently. This can be used either when you are trading live or you are merely practicing. It allows you to know what amount that can be risked.

The trading lot size affects how the market movements can affect the accounts. Let's use an example.

When a 100-pip move occurs, it won't have so much effect on a small trade like similar 100-pip move on a trade size that is quite massive.

As a trader, you will see several lot sizes.

We will explain the lots as follow:

Trading with Micro Lots

The tiniest tradable lots that can be used are called mini lots. A micro lot has a thousand units of the currency that is in your account. If you have funded your account with USD, a micro-lot of that has a value of a thousand dollars, as the base currency.

If you have decided to trade a dollar-based pair, a pip means ten cents.

As a beginner, it is favorable to use micro lots as it reduces your risk, while you practice trading.

Mini lots have ten thousand units of the currency that you use to fund your account. If you are making use of an account that has dollars as its base currency, then every pip in the trade would be valued at around $1.00.

As a beginner that wants to begin with mini lots, it is advisable that you are adequately capitalized.

A dollar per pip may seem quite tiny, but the market sometimes even gets to a hundred pips daily. Sometimes, this may happen in one hour.

If the forex market isn't moving in your direction, this means that you have made a loss of a hundred dollars.

It is you that will choose your ultimate risk tolerance. Before you can trade a mini account, it is advisable that you don't mind using at least two thousand dollars.

Using Standard Lots

A standard lot has a hundred thousand units of the base currency in a trading account. If you have a base currency of dollars, this is a hundred thousand dollar lots. The normal pip size for a standard lot is ten dollars for every pip.

When the trade is against you by ten pip, this is a loss of hundred dollars. This type of lot is used by institutional-sized accounts.

What this translates to is that you should possess at least $25,000 to be able to carry out trades using standard lots.

A lot of forex traders tend to make use of either micro lots or mini lots.

To a novice, this may not seem glamorous, but when you keep the lot size proportional to the size of your account, your trading capital will be preserved, and you can easily trade with it for a long while.

Let's use an illustration;

Using a small trade size compared to what you have in your account can be likened to strolling on a sturdy bridge that has shelter to prevent any issue from worrying you. It doesn't matter if heavy rain occurs; you will be sheltered.

If you place a big trade size when compared to the account funds, it can be likened to walking on a narrow bridge. In this case, the bridge is fragile and narrow, meaning that you can fall at any time. A tiny movement in the market could toss you away, and lead you to a spot that you can't return from.

Below are some things you should consider before you begin.

Do not let your gain become a loss

One thing that has been noticed is that a lot of forex traders tend to turn their profit into a loss. The forex market worldwide does at least $5 trillion daily. This has made it the most significant financial market globally.

The fact that Forex is lucrative has made it popular amongst a lot of traders from novices to experts in the field.

Since it is quite easy to get involved in forex because of the little costs, round-the-clock sessions, and so on, it is also straightforward to lose your capital as you trade forex.

To ensure that your gain doesn't turn to a loss as a forex trader, you should try and avoid some mistakes.

Learn, Learn and Learn

The fact that it is quite easy to get involved in forex has led a lot of people to get involved without bothering to learn. To succeed in forex or any financial market for that matter, you need to learn. You should learn from live trading, experience, as well as reading up on forex literature. Don't forget the news. You spiel find out about economic and geopolitical factors that have effects on the preferred currencies of a trader.

The world of forex is ever changing meaning that you must keep yourself abreast with these changes in the regulations, market conditions, as well as global events.

While you undergo the research process, you should also consider creating a trading plan.

This plan should involve a method where you can screen and analyze investments, in a bid to determine how much risk should be expected when creating investment goals.

Use only a reputable broker

The truth is that the forex world isn't so regulated, unlike others, meaning that you may end up carrying out business with unscrupulous brokers. It is advisable that you only open an account with a National Futures Association (NFA) member if you want your deposits to be safe, and you are interested in the integrity of that broker. Use only brokers that are listed as futures commission merchant with the regulatory body of your country. If the broker isn't registered, avoid them.

It is also advisable that you study the account offerings of the brokers like commissions, leverage amounts, spreads, account withdrawal and funding policies and so on. You can find these out by talking to a customer service representative.

Utilize a practice account

Almost every trading platform out there has a practice account. This is also called a demo account or a simulated account.

The account permits traders to carry out hypothetical trades that do not need a funded account. Using a perceive account allows the trader to get used to order-entry techniques quickly.

Using a practice account allows the trader to learn, thereby avoiding a lot of mistakes in their trading account.

We had seen cases of when a novice trader erroneously adds to a losing position, when he intended to close the trade.

Several errors in the order entry could worsen to a big losing trade. Losing funds is not the only issue; you have to also battle with a stressful and annoying situation.

There is nothing wrong if you decide to try out order entries before you start to place the real money on live trading.

Keep Your Charts clean

When a forex trader creates an account, he or she may be tempted to use every tech assessment tool available in the trading platform.

A lot of these indicators are high in the foreign exchange market, but it is advisable that you reduce the hunger of analysis methods that you use to be efficient.

Making use of several similar kinds of indicators like three oscillators or as three volatility indicators may come off as being unnecessary. Sometimes, you may even get opposite signals. You should try and avoid this.

If you aren't using an analysis technique well, you should consider taking it out of your chart. It is also essential that you look at the total appearance of the workspace.

The hues, kinds and fonts of price hard such as candle bar, line, range bar, and so on that you use should craft out an easy-to-read-and-interpret chart, permitting you to respond to the ever-changing conditions in the market quickly.

Stop Loss Order Is Not Just for Preventing Losses

Stop loss orders are used a lot in preventing losses, but it does more than that. It can also be used in locking profits. If used for this, it is sometimes called a "trailing stop."

At this point, the stop-loss order is being set at a per cent height that is beneath what the current market price is, and different from the price that it was bought at.

The stop loss's price fluctuates the same way the price of the stock adjusts.

What this means is that if the price of a stock increases, you may have to battle with an unrealized gain. This means that you won't have the money with you until after the sales.

Making use of trailing stop permits you to allow your run, and still guarantee you an amount of realized capital gain.

It is important that you note that the stop-loss order will always be a market order, meaning that it would lie low, until the trigger price has been reached. This means that the price your stock may sell for may end up being a bit different from what you specified as your trigger price.

Benefits of stop loss order

One thing that we all love about stop loss is the fact that we don't have to pay a dime to implement it. The normal commission is only charged when you have reached stop-loss price and your stock has been sold. What you should see it as is a free insurance policy.

Using a stop loss ensured that decisions are made based on facts, taking out any form of emotional influence.

Many people end up crushing on their stocks, feeling that if they allowed the stock to stay on, it would surely succeed, even when the facts are saying another story. This leads to delay and procrastination on the part of the trader, and before you know it, he is raking in unimaginable losses.

It doesn't matter what kind of trader you see yourself as; there must be a reason you have decided to own a stock.

The criteria listed by a value investor is usually different from the one listed by a growth investor and an active trader.

Chapter 18: Make Your First Trade

A lot of retail traders operate from a small home office. Others work in regular offices but remain small traders with limited funds but sufficient trading equipment. As a day trader, there is basically no boss or supervisor to tell a trader what to do. Nobody watches over them or bosses them around. This means a trader has the freedom to organize and manage their trading days.

Because of this freedom, day traders need to exercise a lot of discipline. Traders need to wake up early and prepare for the trading day. Mental preparation is part of a trader's morning ritual before, during, or after breakfast. It is advisable to be up a couple of hours before the trading day begins and ensure everything is in place. There are a couple of things that generally need to be achieved.

1. As soon as breakfast is made, the trader should rehearse their strategies in their minds and probably on paper too. Sometimes it is necessary to run a strategy on a demo platform. Also, a good plan should be made and followed to the letter. This plan includes how much money to place on a trade, which points to exit a trade, when to take profits, and so on.

2. Traders need to check and confirm their trading accounts and the amounts therein. It is crucial that a trader knows the amount available for trading purposes so they know the amounts they can spend per trade. It is recommended that traders should not spend more than 2% of their trading capital on a single trade. The accepted range is between 1% and 2% of the account balance. Beginners with no prior trading experience should not spend more than 1% of their trading balance per trade. Also, a trader should exit their positions three minutes prior to a major financial or economic announcement.

3. It is advisable to always or regularly check the financial calendar and note any major events. Any such events should be clearly marked onto the calendar and reminds initiated. These events have major implications for stocks and activity at the markets.

It is crucial that day traders learn how to select the best stocks to trade. This is because the stocks chosen for day trading will pretty much determine the outcome of your trading ventures. As such, choosing the correct stocks ensures that you fare better at the markets and maximize on profitability.

Identifying Stocks for Day Trading

Funds Available

The first instance is to take cognizance of a trader's financial position. Depending on the number of funds available, you can determine the stocks to choose. There is a wide variety of stocks to choose from. However, you can only choose as much as your funds allow you.

You also need to consider the amount of risk you can tolerate. Generally, the amount of risk a trader is willing to take the more they stand to win. Traders also need to consider buying a security in a field or industry that they are familiar with. For instance, an accountant may be happy trading financial stocks while an engineer will be at home with tech stocks, and so on. Such considerations will ensure you understand what is going on in the industry, and this will boost trading ventures.

Liquidity

Traders also need to find securities that are highly liquid and trade in large volumes. There is a reason for this. When a security is trading in high volumes, then it is easy to enter and exit positions. Also, highly liquid securities make it easy to get paid upon exiting a position. Some of the best financial securities that have large volumes and are liquid are blue-chip stocks. These are stocks of highly valued companies that are constantly making large profits, are stable, and considered very valuable.

Stocks that are highly liquid tend to be more easily traded and are easier to discount compared to many others. Also, stocks and securities from firms with large volumes of shares traded tend to be more favorable. Traders should take the time to conduct analysis in order to find which stocks are most suitable. A good stock is one from a large-cap company rather than a low cap firm. This is because it is easier to find buyers of large volume stocks compared with buyers for low volume stocks.

Volatility

Some of the best instruments are highly volatile ones. Volatile stocks and securities provide day traders a chance to capitalize on the rapid and numerous price changes. Remember that day; traders make most of their money due to the rapid or frequent price changes. As such, stocks that are constantly moving up and down or are volatile are much better and preferable compared to less volatile ones.

We have what is known as the TVI or trade volume index. This is a measure of the volumes of a particular stock that is trading at the market. Using this index, traders can determine whether or not to choose the particular stock. TVI indicates the total amount of cash that is following into and out of stock. The volume gives a clear indication of the stock's activity at the markets.

Industry

Another crucial aspect to consider when selecting a stock is the industry. One of the best industries for day traders should be the financial services sector. This sector is excellent because it features most of the above factors like large volumes and volatility. A great example, in this case, is Microsoft Corp. This is a well-established company with a large global market, growing income, and a positive reputation.

Microsoft Corp also happens to be among the most highly traded stocks. This is why it is among the most preferred stock by most day traders. It is definitely an excellent choice for day trading forays as it exhibits all the desired characteristics. Bank of America is a large corporation, it trades a large volume of shares each day, its stock is volatile, yet the bank remains stable and profitable through the years.

Emotions

One important point worth mentioning is that a day trader should never let emotions take charge of trading activities. When a trading strategy is formulated, it should be implemented to the letter. All too often, traders either become greedy or despair and then begin trading guided by their emotions.

For instance, they refuse to exit a winning trade instead of collecting profits first. In other cases, traders choose to continue incurring losses beyond the stop-loss point. These are dangerous attributes and are common among new and novice traders. It is a practice that should be shunned at all costs for successful and profitable day trading.

Summary

Day traders execute various intraday strategies in order to benefit from the volatility at the markets. To be effective, the first step should be the identification of suitable stocks to trade.

There are different stocks available in the market. A good trader will conduct an analysis using tools and charts to find the most appropriate stocks. These are stocks with high volumes from stable companies that showcase a fair amount of volatility.

It does not have to stock only. Day traders can also deal with other commodities such as bonds, currencies, futures, and options. Once the trading instrument has been determined, the only other step is to develop a strategy and begin implementing it. A major challenge that numerous traders experience, especially novice and beginners, is that they let their emotions interfere with their trading. This means that traders take their time to conduct research and come up with a trading strategy only to discard it at the last moment.

Emotional stability is crucial because it is the only way for a trader to execute a strategy and make profits along the way successfully. When emotions take charge, a trader will keep holding on to a falling position beyond the stop-loss point. They will lose money using this approach. However, when winning, they do not take profits as was intended, but instead, they tend to keep at trade and risk losing all their winnings.

Life of a Typical Day Trader

It is commonly believed that the life of a trader is fun and exciting and that they deal in numbers and money all day long. This is far from the truth. A trader's life is not all fun and glam, and they do not really live on the edge. While it is true that they spend the entire trading day dealing in options, stocks, currencies, and other securities, they really do work very hard and tend to focus too much on the markets.

The life of a day trader can actually be exciting simply because of all the numerous events and unexpected occurrences that can take place. But in general, most trading days are quiet with little or no excitement but general trading as usual. There is hardly any action except for reading charts, entering positions, checking news feeds, and so on. Therefore, any glamor that people think exists in day trading is only a figment of the imagination.

You will also find that most day traders, especially small retail traders, trading from their home offices. Many have established a workstation at their home offices from where they do all the work. We also have institutional traders working from fully furnished offices with access to plenty of resources. At any one time, this day, traders will be entering positions in the market and make trades worth hundreds of millions of dollars.

Traders and their Trading Styles

There are different definitions that define traders. For instance, experts sometimes divide traders by the time in which they enter and exit trades. This time is also known as the holding time. At other times, traders can be classified based on the ways in which they identify opportunities and the approach they use to trade these opportunities.

For instance, we have discretionary traders. These are traders who base their trades on decisions based on certain factors. We also have system traders who are named thus because they automate their trades and use the system to execute their strategies. Other kinds of traders are the day trader, swing trader, scalpers, and high-frequency traders. Based on these definitions, it is clear to observe that there is no typical day trader but a variety of different strategies adopted by different day traders.

Chapter 19: Common Day Trading Mistakes to Avoid

Aside from doing the right things, you'll also need to refrain from certain things to succeed as a day trader. Here are some of the most common day trading mistakes you should avoid committing.

Excessive Day Trading

By excessive, I mean executing too many day trades. One of the most common mistakes many newbie day traders make is assuming that they can become day trading ninjas in just a couple of weeks if they trade often enough to get it right. But while more practice can eventually translate into day trading mastery later on, it doesn't mean you can cram all that practice in a very short period of time via very frequent day trading. The adage "the more, the merrier" doesn't necessarily apply to day trading.

Remember, timing is crucial for day trading success. And timing is dependent on how the market is doing during the day. There will be days when day trading opportunities are few and far between and there'll be days when day trading opportunities abound. Don't force trades for the sake of getting enough day trades under your belt.

Even in the midst of a plethora of profitable day trading opportunities, the more the merrier still doesn't apply. Why? If you're a newbie trader, your best bet at becoming a day trading ninja at the soonest possible time is to concentrate on one- or two-day trades per day only. By limiting your day trades, to just one or two, you have the opportunity to monitor and learn from your trades closely.

Can you imagine executing 5 or more trades daily as a newbie and monitor all those positions simultaneously? You'll only get confused and overwhelmed and worse, you may even miss day trading triggers and signals and fail to close your positions profitably.

Winging It

If you want to succeed as a day trader, you need to hold each trading day in reverence and high esteem. How do you do that? By planning your day trading strategies for the day and executing those strategies instead of just winging it.

As cliché as it may sound, failing to plan really is planning to fail. And considering the financial stakes involved in day trading, you shouldn't go through your trading days without any plan on hand. Luck favors those who are prepared and planning can convince lady luck that you are prepared.

Expecting Too Much Too Soon

This much is true about day trading: it's one of the most exciting and exhilarating jobs in the world! And stories many day traders tell of riches accumulated through this economic activity add more excitement, desire, and urgency for many to get into it.

However, too much excitement and desire resulting from many day trading success stories can be very detrimental to newbie day traders. Let me correct myself: it is detrimental to newbie day traders. Why?

Such stories, many of which are probably urban legends, give newbies unrealistic expectations of quick and easy day trading riches. Many beginner day traders get the impression that day trading is a get-rich-quick scheme!

It's not. What many day traders hardly brag about are the times they also lost money and how long it took them to master the craft enough to quit their jobs and do it full time. And even rarer are stories of the myriad number of people who've attempted day trading and failed. It's the dearth of such stories that tend to make day trading neophytes have unrealistic expectations about day trading.

What's the problem with lofty day trading expectations? Here's the problem: if you have very unrealistic expectations, it's almost certain that you'll fail. It's because unrealistic expectations can't be met and therefore, there's zero chances for success.

One of the most unrealistic expectations surrounding day trading is being able to double one's initial trading capital in a couple of months, at most. Similar to such expectations is that of being able to quit one's day job and live an abundant life in just a few months via day trading. Successful day traders went through numerous failures, too, before they succeeded at day trading and were able to do it for a living.

If you decide to give day trading a shot, have realistic expectations. In fact, don't even expect to profit soon. Instead take the initial losses as they come, limiting them through sensible stop-loss limits, and learning from them. Eventually, you'll get the hang of it and your day trading profits will start eclipsing your day trading losses.

Changing Strategies Frequently

Do you know how to ride a bike? If not, do you know someone who does? Whether it's you or somebody you know, learning how to ride a bike wasn't instant. It took time and a couple of falls and bruises along the way.

But despite falls, scratches and bruises, you or that person you know stuck to learning how to ride a bike and with enough time and practice, succeeded in doing so. It was because you or the other person knew that initial failures mean that riding a bike was impossible. It's just challenging at first.

It's the same with learning how to day trade profitably. You'll need to give yourself enough time and practice to master it. Just because you suffered trading losses in the beginning doesn't mean it's not working or it's not for you. It probably means you haven't really mastered it yet.

But if you quit and shift to a new trading strategy or plan quickly, you'll have to start again from scratch, extend your learning time, and possibly lose more money than you would've if you stuck around to your initial strategy long enough to give yourself a shot at day trading successfully or concluding with certainty that it's not working for you.

If you frequently change your day trading strategies, i.e., you don't give yourself enough time to learn day trading strategies, your chances of mastering them become much lower. In which case, your chances of succeeding in day trading becomes much lower, too.

Not Analyzing Past Trades

Those who don't learn history are doomed to repeat it, said writer and philosopher George Santayana. We can paraphrase it to apply to day traders, too: Those who don't learn from their day trading mistakes will be doomed to repeat them.

If you don't keep a day trading journal containing records of all your trades and more importantly, analyze them, you'll be doomed to repeat your losing day trades. It's because by not doing so, you won't be able to determine what you're doing wrong and what you should be doing instead in order to have more profitable day trades than losing ones.

As another saying goes: if you always do what you always did, you'll always get what you always got. Unless you analyze your past day trades on a regular basis, you'll be doomed to repeating the same mistakes and continue losing money on them.

Ditching Correlations

We can define correlations as a relationship where one thing influences the outcome or behavior of another. A positive correlation means that both tend to move in the same direction or exhibit similar behaviors, i.e., when one goes up, the other goes up, too, and vice versa.

Correlations abound in the stock market. For example, returns on the stock market are usually negatively correlated with the Federal Reserve's interest rates, i.e., when the Feds increase interest rates, returns on stock market investments go down and vice versa.

Correlations exist across industries in the stock market, too. For example, property development stocks are positively correlated to steel and cement manufacturing stocks. This is because when the property development's booming, it buys more steel and cement from manufacturing companies, which in turn also increase their income.

Ignoring correlations during day trading increase your risks for erroneous position taking and exiting. You may take a short position on a steel manufacturer's stock while taking a long position on a property development company's stock and if they have a positive correlation, one of those two positions will most likely end up in a loss.

But caution must be exercised with using correlations in your day trades. Don't establish correlations where there's none. Your job is to simply identify if there are observable correlations, what those correlations are, and how strong they are.

Being Greedy

Remember the story of the goose that lay golden eggs? Because the goose's owner was so greedy and couldn't wait for the goose to lay more eggs immediately, he killed the goose and cut it open.

Sadly, for the owner, there were no golden eggs inside the goose because it only created and laid one golden egg every day. His greed caused him to destroy his only wealth-generating asset.

When it comes to day trading, greed can have the same negative financial impact. Greed can make a day trader hold on to an already profitable position longer than needed and result in smaller profits later on or worse, trading losses.

If you remember my story, that was greed in action. Had I been content with the very good returns I already had and closed my position, my paper gains could've become actual gains. I let my greed control my trading and chose to hold on to that stock much longer than I needed to. That trade turned into a losing one eventually.

That's why you must be disciplined enough to stick to your day trading stop-loss and profit-taking limits. And that's why you should program those limits on your platform, too. Doing so minimizes the risks of greed hijacking your otherwise profitable day trades.

Chapter 20: Best Software for Day Trading

A day trading software is a term given to any software that can help in the decision making and analysis in order to make a trade. Some of the software will provide you with accessibility to the tools and all the resources needed.

A day trading software has the following basic features:

- Any software should have the functionality of allowing the setup of trading strategy in the system.
- Possess the order-placing function which is normally automated.
- Tools for continuous assessment of the market developments so as to act on them.

How does trading software works?

Day trading software can be divided into four different categories:

- Charting. Bright day traders will normally chart their prices using different charting software. However, some outside vendors normally offer feeds with charting packages which help in the analysis of technical indicators. Most of these data feeds are normally advanced packages.
- Data. Before any day trader begins trading, you should be aware of the prices of the stocks, its future, and current currencies.
- Execution of trade. After sourcing for the data and analyzed it on a chart, at some point, a day trader will need to enter into trade. Trade execution requires some sort of trading software. A good number of trading software nowadays allow you to develop your own trading strategies using APIs (Application Programming Interface). Some even specifically provide trading capabilities that are automated for day training.

Below are some of the platforms for day trading you can select.

- **Zacks Trade**

Zacks Trade is a brokerage day trading platform mostly for the US and international consumers. It started its trading since 2014 and its offices are suited in Chicago.

This online platform is mostly for active traders and investors. Investors on this trading platform need to make a deposit of around $2500 for them to register an account with the broker. However, if you are seeking help to make a trade, Zacks is the best choice for you since it offers brokerage trades for free. The tradable securities involved on this platform include market stocks, exchange-traded funds, and bonds. On this platform, you can make market trades more than 91 exchanges in different countries.

The cost per share of the commission is around $0.01 with a minimum of $3. This platform is mostly preferred to the active and options traders, investors seeking to trade on foreign stock exchanges and also those who want to access a human broker.

Zacks Trade offers two types of accounts; Zacks Trade Pro normally for the active users and Zacks Trader for the retail traders. Zacks Trader has a simple user interface, therefore, making it easy for the users to navigate through the system.

The pros of this software are that:

- It is quite rare to find a trading platform that offers cheap commission such as a cent. To engage in trading the penny stocks, you will need to pay around 1% of the trade's value with a minimum cost of $3. The cost for options is around $3 for the first contract and cost of additional ones which is 75 cents.
- Zacks normally offers investors with the accessibility to 26 research and 87 reports on subscriptions.
- This software is also available for Linux users. Account-holders can also access Zacks using their mobile phones unlike it is seen on other software.
- Zacks Trade is so safe and secure. Clients normally have their own platforms from the management and they register for their accounts with unique usernames and passwords.
- Good customer service. This platform enables day traders who use their smartphones to trade for a free 24/7-hour basis. It is mostly for traders suited in Asia, the US, and Australia.
- The shortcoming for this software is that it offers slightly higher charges on shares as compared to Interactive brokers.

- **Interactive Brokers**

This software is strongly advisable for advanced and frequent traders. It charges $0.01 per share with no minimum investment required. It offers a wide range of investments such as European bonds for the government and the corporate. Interactive brokers offer research for free to its traders from around 100 providers such as Zacks and many more.

The advantages of this software include:

- The low commission charges on exchange-traded funds and stock tend to favor the frequent traders. The low rates also favor the margin traders.

- Interactive Broker's workstation is fast and offers great features such as watchlists, real-time monitoring, and advanced charting.

- Another great advantage of Interactive Broker is that it offers its traders massive accessibility to research and news services which keeps them up to date.

The greatest shortcoming of Interactive Brokers is that traders find it hard to navigate through the website. This makes it difficult for traders to identify the costs associated with the commissions and fees.

- **TD Ameritrade**

This is one of the largest trading brokerage software with the basic and Thinkorswim platforms. It charges fees of $6.95 per share and no minimum investment is required. The Thinkorswim platform allows clients to customize color schemes and layouts according to their choice of preference. Trade tickets are found on both of the platforms so a trader can enter an order in whichever platform you are using.

After the software development team made updates on the tools and content of this software, there has been an improved look on both of the platforms making it more responsive to the client's devices.

TD Ameritrade offers a range of tradable securities; over 300 exchange-traded funds are free of charge and over 12,000 mutual funds. It also provides investors and traders accessibility to research for good quality trade execution especially for traders using the Thinkorswim platform.

The pros of TD Ameritrade include the following:

- Offers wide news and research abilities to the traders which keep them up to date.

- Provide a full range of investments such as forex and bitcoin futures trading for the right clients.
- Provide massive education support for the traders. There are videos and also articles that provide simple guidelines to the traders on how to use the tools provided. It is so difficult to find a trader who cannot use this software despite you being a guru or a newbie.
- TD Ameritrade offers mock trading accounts. Traders are given virtual money of around $100,000 for practice. Traders can back test trading strategies and access foreign futures.

The biggest shortcoming of TD Ameritrade is the high charges on commission and the exchange-traded funds as compared to other software.

- **Trade Station**

Trade Station is a day training software that charges $5 per share and requires a minimum investment of $500. It normally focuses on good quality data of the market and the trade executions. Its system is well established and normally remains firm during market surges. You can establish your own system using the analysis tools and mock testing strategies provided by this software.

The advantages of this software are as follows:
- The platform has minimal chances of crashing down since it is a stable platform.
- The software feature out excellent charting tools and back testing strategies making it the popular software.
- Education support for this software is at top-notch. It normally offers classes and educational videos to its traders on various topics such as margins and many others.

The shortcoming of this software is that there no cases of forex trading and international trading is limited.

- **eOption**

eOption is another day trading software that focuses on quality. It has a minimum investment of $500 and charges $3 per trade. The massive number of fans of eOption is mostly after the low commission and the extreme faster trade executions.

You can check out the platform before opening the account by using Paper Trading Toolset which is given for free for around 45 days.

This software has various pros:

- is easy for traders to navigate through the web-based platform. The user interface is so simple and the tools provided are easier to be found by the traders.

- Good customer service. The platform is so stable and seldom has cases of crashing down.

- The cost of using this software is very low since the charge per trade is $3. However, users for inactive accounts are normally charged an annual fee of $50.

The cons of this software are:

- Limited accessibility for the traders to research and news providers unlike in other software.
- Education support is not that good. The offerings are limited making it difficult for new traders.

- **Firs trade**

This is a trading software which is free of charge and requires a minimum investment of $0. It began offering $0 commission to traders dealing with options and the stock recently and for its benefit, it offered limited tools and research for the traders using this software. Firs trade also has this lending program which provides lending services to financial bodies and account holders and they can generate income. The traders can even sell the stock with no restrictions.

Some of the pros of this software include the following:

- It provides a set of accounts. It has simplified English, traditional and even Chinese accounts.
- It has lower costs. Charges $0 for the stock and options traders.
- This software provides access to stocks, options and funds type of trading.
- The drawbacks of this software include the following:
- Firs trade does not provide access to forex, future and crypto type of trading.
- It does not have a 24/7 basis for customer support. They only operate in limited hours as compared to other brokerage trading platforms.
- This platform has a few functionalities for its traders. Its traders are forced to use functionality from other platforms.

- **Trading View**

This is a trading software that is free, also has monthly charges of $9.95 for the Pro account, $19.95 for the Pro+ account and $39.95 for the premium account. Trading View does not support stock options and U.S trading.

A trader can make trades on the charts and the software will work out for you the profit and loss reports and analysis.

Its advantages include the following:

- This software is of ease of use even to beginners.
- Offer support for a variety of trades such as stock, forex, and cryptocurrency.
- The charting for this software is easy to use and provides you with various tools.

The disadvantage of this software that turns many off is that it has no real-time news for the traders, unlike other trading software.

Chapter 21: Candlestick Patterns

One of the most popular tools that you'll hear about in trading is the candlestick pattern. The use of candlestick patterns started way back in the 1700s in Japan. The rice traders in Japan started using these patterns to understand market fluctuations so that they can get a better price for their rice in the market.

These patterns are so simple, visually appealing, informative, and easy to understand that they have become the darling of the trading world.

If you are completely new to the market, there is no reason for you to feel intimidated by candlestick patterns. We will discuss them and the way they can help you in understanding the market better.

Body: This is the major part of the candle that represents the opening and closing price of the asset. The whole body of the candle simply represents strength. The farther the opening and closing prices are, the longer would be the body

This body can be represented in Red and Green. The red would mean that the pressure was on the selling side. The green candle would mean that the pressure was on the buying side. Another way to represent the candles is to present them in black and hollow candles. Hollow means buying and black would mean selling pressure.

Wicks: The lines going up and down the candle body are known as the wicks. They denote the high and low an asset made in that particular trading window for which you are looking at it.

Therefore, as you can see, by simply looking at the candles on the screen you can have so much information in front of you in a very visually appealing manner. It is very easy to understand and also helps in the formation of an early trading bias.

On a trading chart, you'll usually see red and green or hollow and black candles side by side or in a specific pattern. These patterns are meaningful. They express the market mood and buying and selling trends.

We classify candlestick patterns into three broad categories.

1. Bullish Candlestick Patterns
2. Bearish Candlestick Patterns
3. Indecisive Candlestick Patterns

We will now discuss them in detail for a better understanding.

Bullish Candlestick Patterns

Hammer

Pattern: This candlestick pattern has a comparatively short body and a longer lower wick giving it a shape of a hammer. You'll find this pattern at the bottom of a downward trend.

This candlestick pattern represents that although there had been a selling pressure in the asset, buyers have started to take interest in it.

Inverse Hammer

Pattern: As the name suggests, this candlestick pattern would be just the opposite of the hammer formation in its shape. It will have a longer wick on the upper side of a short body. It is also found at the bottom of a downward trend.

This pattern also represents that although the sellers have been trying to dominate the market, the buyers are not letting the prices go down and soon the stock price would start moving up.

Piercing Line

Pattern: It will have two red and green candles of almost the same height standing side by side. You will be able to see that the opening price of the second candle would be much higher than the closing price of the first candle.

This candlestick pattern is an indication that the buyers are pushing in and the price of the stock wouldn't keep going down now. It generally represents the reversal of the downtrend in the stock.

Three White Soldiers

Pattern: You'll see stronger and stronger candles standing side by side in an escalating ladder pattern. There would be at least three green or bullish candles. The opening price of each candle would be much higher than the previous one.

This candlestick pattern represents a very strong bullish pattern. This pattern generally emerges after the stock has been on a downtrend for quite some time. It signifies that there is a consistent buying pressure in the stock.

Morning Star

Pattern: This is a three-stick pattern. You'll find a short-bodied star-like pattern between two long red and green candlesticks.

It signifies that the selling pressure has started to ease and the buyers are again showing their interest. This pattern is taken as a symbol of hope in a sinking market and that's why it is called a morning star.

Bullish Engulfing

Pattern: You'll see two candlesticks side by side. The red candlestick representing selling spree would be shorter and the green candlestick would be covering all of it from top to bottom. The green would seem to engulf the red candlestick completely and that's why this pattern is called the Bullish Engulfing Candlestick Pattern.

This candlestick also represents a strong bullish trend and that buying would be heavier than the selling.

Bearish Candlestick Patterns

Hanging Man Pattern

This candlestick pattern would be similar to the hammer pattern in shape like in the bullish candlesticks. The big difference would be that this pattern would appear at the top of the uptrend. From here the trend would reverse and the stock would face more selling pressure making it bearish.

In this candlestick pattern, the highs of the day are very close to the opening levels and the lows are steep. This clearly shows that the sellers are calling the shots that day. It clearly sends a message that the trend in that stock is going to be bearish.

Bearish Engulfing Pattern

You'd again notice this pattern on the uptrend. A small green candle would be completely overshadowed by a thick red candle showcasing the selling pressure. The highs of the green candle would be very near to the opening sessions while the highs and lows on the red candle would be much deeper.

This candlestick pattern speaks of the weakening confidence in the market. It is generally noticed on an uptrend and the stock starts going down from there steeply.

Shooting Star Pattern

The formation of a shooting star is similar to the inverted hammer candlestick. The main difference is in the position where they are formed. The shooting star formation emerges at the top of an uptrend. This formation has a small lower body and a long upper wick.

This candlestick pattern represents that although the buyers tried to push the stock up, they couldn't keep it there. That's the reason the high of the stock is much above the opening price. However, the stock generally remains around its low and closes at that level only. This is a negative signal to the market representing a bearish trend. It appears at the top of an upward trend and from there the stocks usually start making lower lows. This pattern is good for people who are looking for a shorting opportunity in a bearish market.

Evening Star Pattern

This is yet another bearish pattern similar to the morning star pattern in shape and structure. The major difference is that this pattern emerges on an uptrend. You'll find a candle with a very small body and long wicks sandwiched between two long red and green candles. While you'll notice the bullish candle to be thick without greater highs or lows, the bearish candle may show lower lows.

This candlestick pattern clearly indicates a reversal in the bullish trend.

Three Black Crows Pattern

This candlestick pattern clearly shows the stock on a downtrend. It would show at least three red candles on consecutive days. The candles would have a very short wick or no wick at all. This means that the pressure was clearly on selling the stock aggressively. The absence of upper wick shows that there is no enthusiasm in the market in buyers and the stock made no high than its opening price. The selling pressure in the stock would further push it down and that would mean that the stock would open at an even lower price later on.

Indecisive Candlestick Patterns

The candles not only show the market trends but they can also show when the markets are highly indecisive.

Doji Pattern

In this pattern, you'll see that although the stock would achieve higher highs and lower lows, the opening and the closing price would remain in the middle. This means that the pattern wouldn't have a thick body. It would simply look like a plus sign.

This pattern shows that the buying and selling pressure in the stock is in equilibrium. The market is yet not very sure on the side it wants to be at the moment.

It clearly represents a state of indecision.

You'll notice two main kinds of Doji Patterns:

Gravestone Doji Pattern

This kind of pattern would appear when the buyers are trying to push the prices of the stock up, but they are not able to retain it. The Stock would open and close at almost the same price but would make a very higher high. It's low, however, would remain around its open and close.

This pattern shows that although the buyer pressure had been significant, the stock couldn't regain or retain the price levels. It closes around the same price.

Dragonfly Doji Pattern

This candlestick pattern represents that the stock saw a lot of selling pressure but the buyers were able to maintain the same price. It would resemble the capital T sign. The stock would have almost the same opening and closing sign. The stock won't be able to make any high due to the selling pressure and also saw a steep low but the buyers have been successful in maintaining the opening price.

Spinning Top Pattern

This indecision pattern is formed when the buying and selling pressure is mounting and either one of the sides is struggling to gain control of the market.

The shape looks exactly like a spinning top with a short body and long wicks.

Chapter 22: Paper Trading; Practicing Being a Skillful Trader

Before concluding that day trading is challenging for you, you need to understand how it works. Novice traders are often advised to engage in paper trading before anything else. Paper trading refers to a process whereby traders are given the opportunity of trading without using their actual money. In other words, they get to trade by using virtual money provided by their brokers. Since there is no real money involved during paper trading, this gives any trader the opportunity of testing their strategies. If you will be making profits while using paper trading, then there is a good chance that you will also make profits once you begin using your money. Also, a trader can easily make relevant adjustments to their trading strategies to make certain that they make profits from time to time. This section will look into the basics of paper trading. You will be taken through the process of setting up your account. Equally, the pros and cons of paper trading will be outlined for you. From this information, you will know what you are losing out on when you choose not to use a paper trading account.

Significance of Paper Trading

Since you will not be using real money to trade, you must be wondering why it is important for you to engage in paper trading. Paper trading is a fundamental step in your trading experience. It helps you to learn the basics of online trading without putting your money on the line. Therefore, you get to test different trading strategies whether they could work or not. Some of the importance of paper trading you should be aware of are detailed as follows.

Wide Array of Platforms to Use

There is no reason why you should hesitate to paper trade since there are numerous paper trading platforms for you to choose from. This means that it would be relatively easy for you to practice trading. You should do some digging to find out the best paper trading platforms that suit you. A good way of evaluating them is by checking the cool features which are provided. For instance, a feature you should not miss in the platform you use is a tool which will show you how you are performing as compared to other traders. Therefore, with the help of this information, you will know whether you are improving gradually or not.

Learning to Trade with Zero Risks

Essentially, one of the main reasons why you should make good use of paper trading platforms is that they help you learn how to trade with zero risks involved. Consequently, you get to develop some sense of confidence in day trading. One huge mental roadblock faced by most traders is the fear of losing their investments. This prevents most traders from trying to trade. With paper trading, this cannot happen. You will not lose any money. In fact, you will be benefiting from the learning experience you will gain.

No Stress Involved

Traders will have to deal with stress from time to time. When their investments are not performing well, this could have a psychological effect on them. A trader who incurs huge losses consecutively could give up in the process. When one chooses to engage in paper trading, they will be preventing themselves from having to deal with stress. You are new to the trading industry. As such, the last thing you need is some negative vibe proving to you that you cannot be successful in day trading. So, start using a paper trading account to relieve yourself from stress which comes about when traders make trading mistakes.

Build Your Confidence

The confidence you gain in using paper trading accounts is invaluable. At first, you will approach the world of online trading with uncertainty. Well, cut yourself some slack. There is nothing much you know about trading in stocks, forex, and options. As a matter of fact, there are certain terms which could confuse you and you might fail to take advantage of market opportunities when they present themselves. Using paper trading accounts helps you to build confidence as you begin day trading. The assumption that your account is literally growing will motivate you to continue learning. Your focus will be on learning more with the hopes of earning real money in the near future.

You Can Make Mistakes

There is no way you will learn how to trade without making mistakes. In order to become a skillful trader, you have to know the common mistakes which most traders make. In every mistake you make while paper trading, you will be better placed to make the right moves once you use real money. Undeniably, you cannot make the same mistake twice. If a particular move generates losses, you will try your best to avoid it in your next purchases. Also, you might make mistakes while selling your securities. For instance, you could sell too early or late which could affect your financial position. The ability to make mistakes while using a paper trading account makes it essential for any beginner to use it.

Test Strategies That Work

How can you test different strategies if they work when using real money? Testing strategies when you begin trading will only increase your risks. You will run the risk of losing your capital as there are chances that you could make mistakes here and there. Concerning this issue, you need to use a paper trading account to put your strategies to the test. You can test as many strategies as you can. Your main point should be to find one strategy you can implement once you begin trading with real money. Keeping this in mind, new traders should not be afraid of failing. They should not be concerned about making mistakes while paper trading. Honestly, they should make as many mistakes as possible to warrant that they are well exposed to the market trends.

In a word, paper trading could be an excellent platform for novice traders to learn the art of trading. The best part is that they get to experiment without using real money. This infers that there is nothing to lose when using paper trading accounts. You will only lose out on gaining the right trading experience if you choose not to use a paper trading account. Traders should always remember to use the same brokers for their real accounts. Why is this important? Well, using the same broker gives you the confidence that you are not far enough from reality. Consequently, it is vital that you compare options before settling for any broker in the market.

There are several points you need to keep in mind to ensure you make the most out of day trading.

Get Acquainted
Before rushing to trade virtually, you should take steps to familiarize yourself with the platform you will be using. Get to know the common terms which are using in day trading. You don't want to incur losses just because of silly mistakes you ought to have avoided right from the get-go.

Take Notes
When trading virtually, remember that you are doing this to learn how to trade online. Therefore, it makes a lot of sense that you should take notes. Record anything you think that it is important. If there is something that you did not understand, don't move to the next step without clarifying everything. After the markets close, give yourself some time to go over what you learned.

Execute Bad Trades
Don't just trade on good markets. If possible, try and make the wrong decisions and see what happens. The importance of using paper accounts is for you to learn more about the possible mistakes you could make while day trading. Therefore, don't focus on doing everything right. Execute bad trades and learn from them.

Analyze in Sets

The best way of evaluating your performance is by carrying out your analysis in sets. Group your trades in different sets of 10, 20 or 50 and make your evaluation. Doing this helps you know which trades performed well. Accordingly, from the trading strategies which you will be adopting, you will determine the best ones to adopt.

Regardless of the benefits mentioned, there are a few risks involved in paper trading. For that reason, there are traders who would claim that it is not good to start trading by using a demo account.

Euphoria Trading

A big risk involved in paper trading is that a trader might be lured to make certain moves that they wouldn't make in ordinary cases. When they are making huge losses, they might also fail to take their mistakes seriously since there is no money involved in the trading process. This means that a trader might fail to respond in the same manner that they would have done when using real money.

Delayed Data

Traders might fail to gain the real-time data experience that they would have had when using paid accounts. Therefore, delayed data could negatively affect their trading experience. Sadly, there are unscrupulous brokers who might display fake date to their clients. A trader could end up getting the wrong impression about their day trading performance.

Overall, it is imperative to use paper trading bearing in mind that there are many benefits associated with it. There are many signs that could indicate you are a skilled trader. Nonetheless, the best way of knowing that you are surely on the right path is by educating yourself. This makes it vital for you to use a paper trading account.

Chapter 23: Risk Management

Risk management in day exchanging helps cleave down adversities. It can similarly help shield a dealer's record from getting a loss in their cash. When a trader perseveres through a danger zone, there becomes a risk. If it will, in general, be directed, the agent can open oneself up to benefitting in the market.

It is central, yet much of the time, dismissed fundamental to successful dynamic trading. Everything considered a vendor who has made noteworthy advantages can lose it all in just a few terrible trades without a suitable danger the board strategy.

One Percent Rule

Essentially, this standard proposes that one should refrain from investing over 1% of the principal sum for trade. Your tool of trade should not exceed $100 if the trading account has $10000.

This methodology is classic for vendors with records of less than $100,000. Others move higher to more than 2 percent if the expense is dealt with. Various sellers whose records have bigger changes may go with a lower rate. That is because with the portion of the as the size and number of the documentation enlarges. An excellent way to deal with hold your disasters leveled out is to keep the standard underneath 2% any longer, and you'd chance a liberal proportion of your trading account.

Taking in Profit Points

A trader will sell a stock and gather the trade to stop the danger. This is done if at all the trade does not work out in the ways expected by the vendor. The trading locations are supposed to foresee the rate of returns to cut off bad situations before they increase. For example, traders are to sell the stocks immediately if the stock goes down.

The point of taking in the profits is the expense of where a representative will let go of stock and choose the benefit of the exchange. For instance, when a stock is resisting after a period of going up, dealers may need to let it go before association occurs.

The best strategy to efficiently Set Stop-Loss Points

Setting stop setback and take-advantage centers is often done using specific examination, anyway key assessment can similarly accept a key occupation in timing. For instance, when a representative is grasping a stock before salary as enthusiasm manufactures, the individual being referred to might need to release before the market is hit by the news, if wants have ended up being too much high, paying little regard to whether the take advantage cost has been hit.

The moving midpoints address the usual common channels that can deal with these centers because they are definitely not hard to determine and comprehensively pursued by the industry. The main change center joins the 5 to 200-day midpoints. These are applied to the stock diagram to be optimal. These are best set by applying them to a stock's diagram and choosing if the stock expense has reacted to them in the past as either an assistance or resistance level.

Assistance or obstacle example lines are another great style to reduce a backward level. These can be set by traders who have gone over the top and bottom on the great volume. Just as changing centers, the overall is to choose points where the value coincides with the lines and on the same intensity.

When Setting these centers, here are some key things

You are to use the central points that go for long time consistent stocks to reduce the presently available opening that is priced to stop the danger.

Change the central points to be equal with the value. For instance, the goal has to use the many points to reduce the made signs.

Reduce the backlog to less than 1.5 times on the current capriciousness, as it is too focus even to consider evening consider getting executed without reason.

Modify the stop incident, as demonstrated by the market's eccentrics. In case the stock price is not changing much for the better, then the danger centers can be corrected.

Use alluded to important functions. For instance, there are advantages set out as time moves forward, as key time spans to be in or out of a trade as unconventionality and powerlessness can arise.

Learning Possible Return

Setting stop incidents and receive advantage centers are, moreover, essential to learning the typical return. Due to the noteworthiness of the figuring can't be misrepresented, as it powers shippers to consider their trades and reason them completely. These give a conscious technique to regard various trades and choose the best one.

Grow and Hedge

When you are guaranteed an advantage however much as could reasonably be expected from your trading infers never putting your eggs in a solitary bushel. In case you invest all your cash in one stock, these sets you up for your setting yourself up for a foreseen setback. So, make a point to expand your hypotheses. Notwithstanding the way that this encourages you to take care of the danger, anyway, it furthermore increases your possibilities.

You can also get yourself when you need to assistance your spot. When the outcome is stable, you should focus on the spot of the stock. You can also consider going the different side through options which can make you sure of your location. During the going down of a trade, you can ask for help.

End on hazard the board

Sellers should reliably be aware when they plan to come in or exit a trade before acting on it. By using stop disasters reasonably, a representative can confine incidents just as the events a trade is left superfluously. Considering, make your battle course of action early, so you'll unquestionably acknowledge you've won the war.

Market Cap Vs. Float

Market cap depends on the complete estimation of each of the organization's portions of stock. The float is the number of offers really accessible for exchanging. A buoy is determined by subtracting firmly held offers - possessed by insiders, workers, the organization's Employee Stock Ownership Plan or other major long-haul investors - from the complete offers remarkable. At the correct cost, obviously, the firmly held offers may begin to drift. Interesting how that functions.

Market capitalization alludes to the all-out estimation of every one of them an organization's portions of stock. It is determined by duplicating the cost of a stock by its complete number of extraordinary offers. For instance, an organization with 20 million offers selling at $50 an offer would have a market top of $1 billion.

For what reason is to advertise capitalization such a significant idea? It enables financial specialists to comprehend the general size of one organization versus another. Market top estimates what an organization is worth on the open market, just as the market's view of its future prospects since it reflects what financial specialists are eager to pay for its stock.

Enormous top organizations are ordinarily firms with a market estimation of $10 at least a billion. Huge top firms frequently have a notoriety for delivering quality products and enterprises, a background marked by predictable profit installments, and enduring development. They are regularly predominant players inside built-up enterprises, and their image names might be recognizable to a national shopper crowd. Accordingly, interests in huge top stocks might be viewed as more traditionalist than interests in the little top or mid-top stocks, possibly presenting less hazard in return for less forceful development potential.

Mid-top organizations usually are organizations with a market an incentive between $2 billion and $10 billion. Ordinarily, these are set up organizations in businesses encountering or expected to encounter quick development. These medium-sized organizations might be expanding a piece of the pie and improving by and large intensity. This phase of development is probably going to decide if an organization, in the long run, satisfies its maximum capacity. Mid-top stocks by and large fall between enormous tops and little tops on the hazard/return range. Mid-tops may offer more development potential than huge tops, and perhaps less hazard than little tops.

Little top organizations are regularly those with a market estimation of $300 million to $2 billion. For the most part, these are youthful organizations that serve specialty showcases or developing ventures. Little tops are considered the most forceful and hazardous of the 3 classifications. The generally constrained assets of little organizations can conceivably make them progressively powerless to a business or monetary downturn. They may likewise be helpless against the extreme challenge and vulnerabilities normal for untried, prospering markets. Then again, little top stocks may offer noteworthy development potential to long haul financial specialists who can endure unpredictable stock value swings for the time being.

What could affect an organization's market Cap?

There are a few factors that could affect an organization's market top. Huge changes in the estimation of the offers—either up or down—could affect it, as could change in the number of offers issued. Any activity of warrants on an organization's stock will expand the number of extraordinary offers, accordingly weakening its current worth. As the activity of the warrants is normally done underneath the market cost of the offers, it could possibly affect the organization's market top.

In any case, the showcase top normally isn't modified as the consequence of a stock split or a profit. After a split, the stock cost will be diminished since the quantity of offers remarkable has expanded. For instance, in a 2-for-1 split, the offer cost will be divided. Even though the quantity of remarkable offers and the stock value change, an organization's market top stays steady. The equivalent applies to a profit. On the off chance that an organization issues a profit hence expanding the number of offers held—its value generally drops.

To manufacture a portfolio with a legitimate blend of little top, mid-top, and enormous top stocks, you'll have to assess your budgetary objectives, hazard resistance, and time skyline. An expanded portfolio that contains an assortment of market tops may help lessen speculation chance in any one zone and bolster the quest for your long-haul money related objectives.

Chapter 24: Retail Vs Institutional Traders

Retail traders are individuals who can be either part-time or full traders but don't work for a firm, and are not managing funds from other people. These traders hold a small percentage of the volume in the trade market.

On the other hand, institutional traders are composed of hedge funds, mutual funds, and investment banks who are often armed with advanced software, and are usually engaged in high-frequency trading.

Nowadays, human involvement is quite minimal in the operations of investment firms. Backed up by professional analysts and huge investments, institutional investors can be quite aggressive.

So, at this point, you might be wondering how a beginner like you can compete against the big players?

Our advantage is the freedom and flexibility we enjoy. Institutional traders have the legal obligation to trade. Meanwhile, individual traders are free to trade or to take a break from trading if the market is currently unstable.

Institutional traders should be active in the market and trade huge volumes of stocks regardless of the stock price. Individual traders are free to sit out and trade if there are possible opportunities in the market.

But sadly, most retail traders do not possess the know-how in identifying the right time to be active and the best time to wait. If you want to be profitable in day trading, you need to eliminate greed and develop patience.

The biggest problem of losers in day trading is not the size of their accounts or the lack of access to technology, but their sheer lack of discipline. Many are prone to bad money management and over-trading.

Some retail traders are successful by following the guerilla strategy, which refers to the unconventional approach to trading derived from guerilla warfare. Guerilla combatants are skilled in using hit-and-run tactics like raids, sabotage, and ambushes to manipulate a bigger and less-mobile conventional opponent.

The US military is considered as one of the strongest armies in the modern world. But this mighty force suffered humiliation caused by the guerilla warfare used by North Vietnam during the Vietnam War.

Following this analogy, guerilla trading involves waiting or hiding until you are ready to grab an opportunity to win small battles in the financial warfare. This can help you gain fast revenue while minimizing your risk.

Remember, your mission is not to defeat institutional traders. Instead, you should focus on waiting for the right opportunity to earn your target income.

As a retail trader, you can make profits from market volatility. It can be impossible to make money if the markets are flat. Only institutional traders have the tools, expertise, and money to gamble in such circumstances.

You must learn how to choose stocks that can help you make fast decisions to the downside or upside in a predictable approach. On the other hand, institutional traders follow high frequency trading, which allows them to profit from very small price movements.

As a retail trader, you should only work in the retail domain the advantage of retail trading is that other retail traders also use them. The more traders use these strategies, the better they can work.

As more traders learn effective stock market strategies, more people will join the market so more stocks will move up faster. The more players in the market, the faster it will move. This is the reason why it is important for successful traders to share their strategies. This will not only help other traders to become more profitable, but it can also increase the number of traders who are using proven strategies.

There's no benefit in hiding these strategies or keeping them secret. In computer-aided trading, most of the stocks will follow the trend of the market, unless there's a good reason not to follow. Therefore, when the market is rising, most stocks will also move up. If the overall market is declining, the prices of the stocks will also decline.

But you should also bear in mind that there will be a handful of stocks that can go against the grain because they have a catalyst.

But for a brief overview, Alpha Predators are what retail traders are hunting for. These stocks usually tank when the markets are running, and they run when the markets are tanking.

It is generally okay if the market is running, and the stocks are running as well. Just be sure that you are trading stocks that are moving because they have a valid reason to move, and are not just moving with the general market conditions.

Probably, you are wondering what the basic catalyst for stocks is to make them ideal for day trading.

Here are some catalysts:

- Debt offerings
- Buybacks
- Stock splits
- Management changes
- Layoffs
- Restructuring
- Major contract wins / losses
- Partnerships / alliances
- Major product releases
- Mergers and / or acquisitions
- FDA approval / disapproval
- Earnings surprises
- Earnings reports

Retail traders who are engaged in reversal trades usually choose stocks that are selling off because there has been some bad press about the company. Whenever there's a fast sell-off because of bad press, many traders will notice and begin monitoring the stock for what is called a bottom reversal.

It can be difficult to perform a reversal trade if the stocks are trending down with the overall market like what happened to oil several years ago. The stock value increases by 20 cents and you may think it is a reversal. Then they are quickly sold off for another 60 cents. The sell-off is happening because the stocks are getting bad press.

For a while, oil was a weak sector and the majority of the energy and oil stocks were selling off. If a sector is weak, then it is not a good time for a reversal trade. This is where you need to identify the reason behind any significant movement in the market.

In order to do that, you need to remember the fourth rule in day trading:

Rule No. 4 - Always ask: is this stock moving because the general market is moving, or there's a unique catalyst behind this movement?

Research is crucial at this point. As you gain experience as a day trader, you will need to identify the difference between general market trends and catalyst-based movements. As a day trader, you need to be careful that you are not on the wrong side of the trade, and going against institutional traders.

How can you do that?

Stay away from trading stocks that are not getting enough attention. You will be in a sandbox doing your own thing. Go where everyone else is going. Concentrate on the stocks that are moving every day and are getting attention from retail traders.

Are blue-chip stocks like IBM, Coca-Cola, or Apple ideal for retail traders? You can try, but you need to remember that these are slow-paced stocks, which are heavily dominated by algorithmic traders and institutional traders. Plus, they are often very hard to trade.

How can you identify the stocks that are alluring retail traders? There are some proven ways to do this.

First, you can use day trading stock scanners. Basically, the stocks that are significantly moving up or down are the stocks that are being monitored by retail traders.

Second, find online community groups or social media groups where retail traders hang out. Twitter and Stock Twits are often good places to learn what is currently trending. If you regularly follow successful traders, then you may see for yourself what everyone is following. There's a big advantage to being part of a community of day traders.

You can read the insights of traders and the specific stocks they are considering. If you are a lone trader, then you may be out of touch in the market. You will just make it difficult for yourself because you will not know where the action is.

Chapter 25: Portfolio Diversification

Day traders generally execute trades in the course of a single trading day while investors buy and hold stocks for days, weeks, months, and sometimes even a couple of years. In between these two extremes are other forms of trading. These include swing trading and position trading, among others.

Swing trading is where a trader buys an interest in a commodity or stock and holds the position for a couple of days before disposing of it. Position trading, on the other hand, is where a trader buys a stake in a commodity or stock for a number of weeks or even several months. While all these trades carry a certain element of risk, day trading carries the biggest risk.

A trader with the necessary skills and access to all the important resources is bound to succeed and will encounter a steep learning curve. Professional day traders work full time, whether working for themselves or for large institutions. They often set a schedule which they always adhere to. It is never wise to be a part-time day trader, a hobby trader, or a gambler. To succeed, you have to trade on a full-time basis and be as disciplined as possible.

Diversification is considered an effective risk management technique. It is widely used by both traders and investors. The gist behind this approach is that investing funds in just single security is extremely risky as the entire trade could potentially go up in smoke or incur significant losses.

An ideal portfolio of securities is expected to fetch a much higher return compared to a no-diversified portfolio. This is true even when compared to the returns of lower risk investments like bonds. Generally, diversification is advisable not only because it yields better returns but also because it offers protection against losses.

Diversification Basics

Traders and investors put their funds in securities at the securities markets. One of the dangers of investing in the markets is that traders are likely to hold onto only one or two stocks at a time. This is risky because if a trade was to fail, then the trader could experience a catastrophe. However, with diversification, the risk is spread out so that regardless of what happens to some stocks, the trader still stands to be profitable.

At the core of diversification is the challenge posed by unsystematic risks. When some stocks or investments perform better than others, these risks are neutralized. Therefore, for a perfectly balanced portfolio, a trader should ensure that they only deal with assets that are non-correlated. This means that the assets respond in opposite ways or differently to market forces.

The ideal portfolio should contain between 25 and 30 different securities. This is the perfect way of ensuring that the risk levels are drastically reduced and the only expected outcomes are profitability.

In summary, diversification is a popular strategy that is used by both traders and investors. It makes use of a wide variety of securities in order to improve yield and mitigate against inherent and potential risks.

It is advisable to invest or trade in a variety of assets and not all from one class. For instance, a properly diversified portfolio should include assets such as currencies, options, stocks, bonds, and so on. This approach will increase the chances of profitability and minimize risks and exposure. Diversification is even better if assets are acquired across geographical regions as well.

Best Diversification Approach

Diversification focuses on asset allocation. It consists of a plan that endeavors to allocate funds or assets appropriately across a variety of investments. When an investor diversifies his or her portfolio, then there is some level of risk that has to be accepted. However, it is also advisable to devise an exit strategy so that the investor is able to let go of the asset and recoup their funds. This becomes necessary when a specific asset class is not yielding any worthwhile returns compared to others.

If an investor is able to create an aptly diversified portfolio, their investment will be adequately covered. An adequately diversified portfolio also allows room for growth. Appropriate asset allocation is highly recommended as it allows investors a chance to leverage risk and manage any possible portfolio volatility because different assets have varying reactions to adverse market conditions.

Investor opinions on diversifications

Different investors have varying opinions regarding the type of investment scenarios they consider being ideal. Numerous investors believe that a properly diversified portfolio will likely bring in a double-digit return despite prevailing market conditions. They also agree that in the worst-case situation will be simply a general decrease in the value of the different assets. Yet with all this information out there, very few investors are actually able to achieve portfolio diversification.

So why are investors unable to simply diversify their portfolios appropriately? The answers are varied and diverse. The challenges encountered by investors in diversification include weighting imbalance, hidden correlation, underlying devaluation, and false returns, among others. While these challenges sound rather technical, they can easily be solved. The solution is also rather simple. By hacking these challenges, an investor will then be able to benefit from an aptly diversified platform.

There are different ways of allocating investments to assets. According to studies, most investors, including professional investors, portfolio managers, and seasoned traders actually rarely beat the indexes within their preferred asset class. It is also important to note that there is a visible correlation between the performance of an underlying asset class and the returns that an investor receives. In general, professional investors tend to perform more or less the same as an index within the same class asset.

Investment returns from a diversified portfolio can generally be expected to imitate the related asset class closely. Therefore, asset class choice is considered an extremely crucial aspect of an investment. In fact, it is the single more crucial aspect for the success of a particular asset class. Other factors, such as individual asset selection and market timing, only contribute about 6% of the variance in investment outcomes.

Wide Diversifications between Various Asset Classes Diversification to numerous investors simply implies spreading their funds through a wide variety of stocks in different sectors such as health care, financial, energy, as well as medium caps, small, and large-cap companies. This is the opinion of your average investor. However, a closer look at this approach reveals that investors are simply putting their money in different sectors of stocks class. These asset classes can very easily fall and rise when the markets do.

A reliably diversified portfolio is one where the investor or even the manager is watchful and alert because of the hidden correlation that exists between different asset classes. This correlation can easily change with time, and there are several reasons for this. One reason is international markets. Many investors often choose to diversify their portfolios with international stocks.

However, there is also a noticeable correlation across the different global financial markets. This correlation is clearly visible not just across European markets but also emerging markets from around the world. There is also a clear correlation between equities and fixed income markets, which are generally the hallmarks of diversification.

This correlation is actually a challenge and is probably a result of the relationship between structured financing and investment banking. Another factor that contributes to this correlation is the rapid growth and popularity of hedge funds. Take the case where a large international organization such as a hedge fund suffers losses in a particular asset class.

Should this happen, then the firm may have to dispose of some assets across the different asset classes. This will have a multiplier effect as numerous other investments, and other investors will, therefore, be affected even though they had diversified their portfolios appropriately. This is a challenge that affects numerous investors who are probably unaware of its existence. They are also probably unaware of how it should be rectified or avoided.

Realignment of Asset Classes

One of the best approaches to solving the correlation challenge is to focus on class realignment. Basically, asset allocation should not be considered as a static process. Asset class imbalance is a phenomenon that occurs when the securities markets develop, and different asset classes exhibit varied performance.

After a while, investors should assess their investments then diversify out of underperforming assets and instead shift this investment to other asset classes that are performing well and are profitable in the long term. Even then, it is advisable to be vigilant so that no one single asset class is over-weighted as other standard risks are still inherent. Also, a prolonged bullish market can result in overweighting one of the different asset classes which could be ready for a correction. There are a couple of approaches that an investor can focus on, and these are discussed below.

Diversification and the Relative Value

Investors sometimes find asset returns to be misleading, including veteran investors. As such, it is advisable to interpret asset returns in relation to the specific asset class performance. The interpretation should also take into consideration the risks that this asset class is exposed to and even the underlying currency.

When diversifying investments, it is important to think about diversifying into asset classes that come with different risk profiles. These should also be held in a variety of currencies. You should not expect to enjoy the same outcomes when investing in government bonds and technology stocks. However, it is recommended to endeavor to understand how each suits the larger investment objective.

Using such an approach, it will be possible to benefit more from a small gain from an asset within a market where the currency is increasing in value. This is as compared to a large gain from an asset within a market where the currency is in decline. As such, huge gains can translate into losses when the gains are reverted back to the stronger currency. This is the reason why it is advisable to ensure that proper research and evaluation of different asset classes are conducted.

Currencies should be considered

Currency considerations are crucial when selecting asset classes to diversify in. take the Swiss franc for instance. It is one of the world's most stable currencies and has been that way since the 1940s. Because of this reason, this particular currency can be safely and reliably used to measure the performance of other currencies.

However, private investors sometimes take too long choosing and trading stocks. Such activities are both overwhelming and time-consuming. This is why, in such instances, it is advisable to approach this differently and focus more on the asset class. With this kind of approach, it is possible to be even more profitable. Proper asset allocation is crucial to successful investing. It enables investors to mitigate any investment risks as well as portfolio volatility. The reason is that different asset classes have different reactions to all the different market conditions.

Constructing a well-thought out and aptly diversified portfolio, it is possible to have a stable and profitable portfolio that even outperforms the index of assets. Investors also have the opportunity to leverage against any potential risks because of different reactions by the different market conditions.

Chapter 26 - The 3 M's of Trading

Mindset

Of all the skills that you must master, having the proper mindset to trade is the most important. 90% of your success will come from your ability to trade Forex with discipline.

There is a substantial difference between simulated trading and actual forex trading from a psychological standpoint. When you trade in simulation, the brain applies 100% logic. Emotion plays no part and has no effect. Therefore, achieving 15 days of consecutive success on a demo account is achieved by simply following the trading rules. When you start trading with real money, a whole new range of issues suddenly comes into play.

It is vitally important that you fully understand the emotional side of trading before you ever consider trading real money. When you go from simulation trading to trading real money, the brain will apply only 10% logic and replace the other 90% with emotion. It's as if suddenly two "devils" jumped upon your shoulders...two devils named "Fear" and "Greed" and they always tell you to do opposite things.

When you are not in the market, Fear says, "Stay out!" and Greed says, "Get in!". When you are in the market, Greed says "Stay in!" and Fear says, "Get out!".

Both of these devilish emotions pulling you in opposite directions at the same time creates uncertainty in the traders mind.

Suppose we put a two-foot wide lumber that is twenty feet long on the floor in a room and we asked you to walk from one end to the other as quickly as you can. You would confidently go from one end to the other in a matter of seconds with no difficulty.

Now, if we put the same piece of lumber on top of the 50th floor between two buildings and asked you to cross it, how long do you think it would take you now? You would probably never even try because fear would be telling you could fall. Is that fear based on the fact that you suddenly forgot how to walk?

No, it's based on your fear of falling. Just as the fear of falling applies in this example, the fear of losing applies to the trader using real money. How do we learn to overcome these fears? What if we simply raised the lumber off the floor only one inch and we had you cross it over and over until you were completely confident then raised it another inch, etc., etc. We would eventually reach a point where the lumber would be 50 stories high and you could still cross it with confidence because you learned how to ignore your fear emotion through a controlled step-by-stop process.

This is why simulation trading is so important in the process of becoming a successful trader. Step-by-step you gain confidence in yourself and your trading method. This confidence is vital. Even after completing your simulation trading with 15 consecutive days of profit, do not begin trading real money with large amounts. As with the lumber example, you will want to inch into the market with the smallest amount...only one E-mini contract per trade. By doing this, you are able to put your discipline on trial, so to speak, with the least amount of capital risk involved.

Once important consideration is the fact that you must never trade with capital that you cannot afford to lose. It is extremely difficult for the trader to trade unemotionally when he is constantly in fear of losing money he cannot afford to lose.

No one ever likes to lose. We must accept the fact that taking a loss is, and always will be, a part of trading forex. It's how we deal with those losses that affects our ability as traders to trade effectively on a long-term basis. You must be willing to accept stop outs as a cost of doing business, not loss, as long as that it was based on following correct trading rules. As an example, imagine you are the owner of a very profitable store.

As a business owner, you know that there will be those inevitable bills to pay...employees, utilities, insurance, rent, etc. You pay them without thinking about them as a loss. They are merely the cost of doing business. This is exactly how you must think of the occasional trade stop outs. It's going to happen and you should simply put it behind you and go on to the next trade.

Never let the result of one trade affect how you feel about entering another one. If a stop out in one trade causes you to hesitate taking the next trade you should be aware that you are now trading emotionally instead of logically. Reacting to the market and chasing it in order to "get even" are sure signs of emotional trading and certain to go bad very quickly. Steps must be taken immediately to correct this emotional reaction. Accept the inevitable stop out as just a cost of doing business as long as it is based on correctly trading the method and as long as the overall results are positive.

If you have made a trading mistake, then you must take the necessary steps to insure the mistake is not repeated. There are not many different mistakes that you can make so make the commitment to learn how to recognize them and correct them immediately.

Here is a good effective strategy that will help you stay unemotional in the market: First, when you take a trade, make sure that it is based on your trading method and that you are not violating any trading rules. Next is to be prepared mentally for the worst-case scenario (getting stopped out) by accepting the loss already in your mind as you enter each trade. By accepting the possible loss, the fear of being stopped out is removed and, since there is nothing else to fear, you can then trade with total logic and no emotion.

Since trading is 90% a mental exercise, getting in the right mindset erases the emotion and lets the logic do its work. The best mindset is to actually feel positive and good about a stop out (as long as it was not the result of a mistake) because it means you did your job correctly and cut your loss short and now that trade is behind you.

There is another consideration that is somewhat the reverse of losing. Sometimes traders experience a period of extended winnings and this causes them to become overconfident and start taking wild risks and abandoning their rules. This is not to be confused with trading aggressively. You can be aggressive and still trade by your rules. But senseless risk taking is a common story you hear of people who were once winners, but went home with empty pockets.

Money Management

Always be sure to place a protective stop loss order immediately after entering the market. Having an actual protective stop loss order, in the market should not allow a substantial loss in a single trade.

As a rule, you should never risk more than 5% of your trading capital in any single trade.

The best way of doing this type of day trading is by setting a weekly goal. If you set a weekly goal such as 100 pips, which is way below the weekly average result, it becomes easy to achieve that very reasonable goal on a consistent basis.

As you start experiencing the consistency in achieving your weekly profit goals, you will want to inevitably increase your weekly profit goals. The best way to do this is to add more lots based on the money management concept explained below. Trying to trade more to make more points in order to increase the profit, is not the right way.

The best way to manage your trading capital and risk is to base it upon your results. As you begin trading with one mini contract, withdraw some percentage of your profit to reward yourself and leave the remainder in your trading account. The percentages will vary depending upon your needs.

As you are rewarding yourself, you are also building up your trading capital to the point where you have enough margin to add one more contract to your trades. (Remember, just because you have the margin to trade more contracts, you should NOT allow yourself to violate the 5% capital risk rule).

We cannot over emphasize the importance of never trading with capital that you cannot afford to lose.

Methodology

Trade and learn powerful methodology. Attend live training webinar each month. You may also consider one-on-one training. Never hesitate to email me to a veteran and knowledgeable if you are having a problem understanding trades. Just remember that you should generate at least four weeks of profitable trading in simulation first before actual trading. Otherwise, your chance of success will be close to zero.

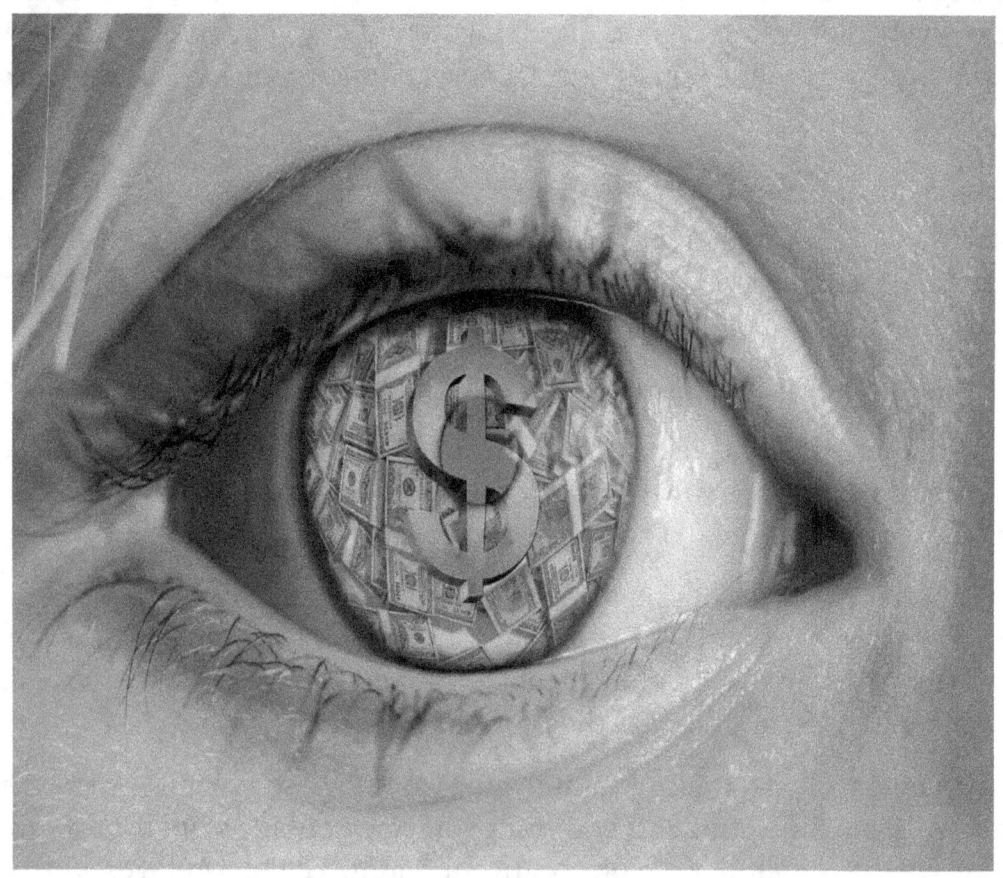

Conclusion

Trading is a tough endeavor to undertake but there's no need to complicate it needlessly. By following a structured approach, you too can realize the immense potential it has to improve your life. You might be wondering about exit opportunities and about how capital raising works?

Generally, I would advise beginners to not worry about this just yet. Once you have the results, capital will come. However, there is the danger of you risking far too much capital due to not realizing the amount of investment capital you can potentially raise. Everyone gets into trading for the money and freedom potential it provides in our lives, so it is unwise to ignore it.

If you can follow strict risk limits and guidelines to an institutional level, you can have your trading account audited and use this as part of a job application to hedge funds or to proprietary trading firms (prop shops.) Truth be told, it won't be easy to land a trading position at a hedge fund, but prop shops are more than accommodating of traders who have a good track record.

In addition to this, there are trading incubators, the most famous being Axiselect, which is run by the Australian broker Axitrader which helps traders' transition over a three to five-year period from a retail trading platform to an institutional level ("Trading Incubation Program", 2020). They will help you raise money and will shop your track record around for you, so you don't need to worry about sinking your life savings into trading in order for you to make money.

Institutions look primarily at risk adjusted returns and anything between a 10-20% yearly return is considered stellar, with monthly drawdowns of less than 3%. Those numbers might sound low but consider that you'll be risking very little to be able to stay under the drawdown limit.

So, don't worry about not having enough capital to be able to get rich. As I said, if you can trade well and properly, capital will find you. Trading is one of the few remaining endeavors where you can truly make millions purely on the basis of your abilities.

You don't need to apply all that you've learned at once. Take baby steps, one at a time. The important thing is you start building momentum. The longer you put off action, the higher your risks are for failure.

Always keep in mind that you'd be better off starting your day trades by practicing on your chosen trading platform's simulator. That way, you get to experience real time trading without losing money. At least, you already have experience by the time you start trading your own money, which may minimize your initial trading risks.

Trading can be an intimidating topic, but as you may notice by now it is certainly not challenging to engage in once you know what you are doing. Although the stakes may seem higher because they involve cash money, the consensus remains the same: if you continue to educate yourself on how to make this strategy work and you continue honing your skills, it will become easier. The financial markets are full of abundance and all you have to do is work to achieve all of it! I wish you the best of luck with your trading.

www.ingramcontent.com/pod-product-compliance
Lightning Source LLC
Chambersburg PA
CBHW080458220526
45465CB00006B/2305